EXPLORE THE CRYPTO UNIVERSE AND TRADE SAVVY

FOR THE NOVICE AND EXPERT. DEFINING DEFI. ALTCOINS.STABLECOINS. TOKENS. NFTS. WEB3. BRIDGING. STAKING. METAVERSE

various sources. Please consult a licensed professional before attempting any techniques outlined in this book.

By reading this book, the reader agrees that under no circumstances is the author responsible for any direct or indirect losses incurred due to the use of the information within this book, including, but not limited to, errors, omissions, or inaccuracies.

This book is dedicated to everyone who has made lots, lost lots, and could have made lots of money because of timing. Many investors who began this journey without awareness lost their bitcoins and crypto wallets. This book is dedicated to you and future investors of cryptocurrencies.

TABLE OF CONTENTS

Introduction

In 2013, a single Bitcoin was worth around $100. Fast forward a decade, and its value has soared to unimaginable heights, surpassing $60,000 at times. This dramatic rise isn't just about numbers. It implies a shift in the financial landscape. Cryptocurrencies, once a niche interest for tech enthusiasts, have exploded into mainstream consciousness. They are reshaping how we interpret money, investment, and even the concept of value itself. However, it's important to note that the crypto market has risks. Volatility, security concerns, and regulatory changes are all factors that can impact your investments. But with these risks come opportunities for significant financial growth.

The purpose of this book is clear: to guide you through this rapidly evolving crypto universe. Whether you're just starting or have been trading for years, this book aims to empower you with the knowledge and tools needed to navigate the digital financial landscape. We will explore conservative and aggressive trading strategies, helping you find your path in the diverse digital currency world.

Allow me to introduce myself. I'm Rogelio Beltran, a cryptocurrency trader since May 2021. In these few years, I've witnessed the incredible capacity of digital currencies and the blockchain technology that supports them. My journey has been one of constant learning and adaptation, experiencing both the highs of successful trades and the lows of market downturns. This book is my effort to share that understanding with you based on my experiences and insights.

As we move closer to a digital future, cryptocurrency education becomes more critical than ever. It's not just about making money; it's about understanding a new form of financial interaction. By being informed, you position yourself to make better decisions in trading and investing in digital assets and to recognize opportunities and risks in a changing world.

This book is structured to cover an expansive range of topics, providing a comprehensive learning of the crypto landscape. We'll start with the basics, defining key terms like DeFi, altcoins, stablecoins, and tokens. We'll explore the intricacies of staking and how to earn passive income. You'll learn to choose a reliable exchange and securely use digital wallets like MetaMask and Trust Wallet. We'll also discuss the potential of emerging technologies like Web3, which is the next evolution of the internet that is decentralized and user-centric, and the Metaverse. Users can interact with a computer-generated environment and other users in this virtual reality space. Each chapter builds on the last, ensuring you thoroughly understand the crypto universe.

Our target audience includes young adults new to managing their finances, adults over 18, and those nearing retirement looking to diversify their portfolios. Each group brings a unique perspective, and this book is designed to address their specific needs and interests. Whether you want to start small or make significant investments, there's something here for everyone.

So, what can you expect to gain from this book? You'll walk away with practical strategies for trading cryptocurrency. You'll clearly understand the terms and technologies that define this space. You'll learn how to build a retirement portfolio using cryptocurrency, leveraging extra funds you don't need for immediate expenses. Most importantly, you'll be confident to make informed decisions in an increasingly digital world.

As we conclude this introduction, I invite you to approach your cryptocurrency journey curiously. Be open to learning and ready to adapt. The chapters ahead offer a wealth of knowledge and insights. Let them guide you, inspire you, and challenge you. Your adventure in the crypto universe begins here. Welcome aboard.

Chapter 1: Understanding the Crypto Basics

In 2021, the crypto market reached an astonishing peak of $2.9 trillion. This isn't just a staggering figure to marvel at; it marks a pivotal point in how we perceive and interact with money. The rise of crypto isn't just about Bitcoin or Ethereum. It's about a broader wave of innovation known as Decentralized Finance, or DeFi, which promises to revolutionize how we handle financial transactions. Understanding the fundamental concepts is crucial as we stand on the brink of this digital transformation. This chapter lays the groundwork by exploring these basic yet powerful ideas, offering you the insight needed to navigate this complex landscape.

1.1 Demystifying DeFi: What It Means and Why It Matters

Decentralized Finance, or DeFi, represents a monumental shift from traditional financial systems to a more open, inclusive, and efficient model. At its core, DeFi leverages blockchain technology to eliminate intermediaries like banks and brokers, enabling direct, peer-to-peer financial transactions. This decentralization is not just a change; it's a transformation. Financial transactions no longer require trust from a central authority. Instead, they rely on smart contracts—self-executing contracts coded to enforce and execute agreements without human intervention. This automation subjugates human error and fraud risk, providing transparency and security not found in the traditional financial system. Additionally, DeFi offers open access, allowing anyone with an internet connection to partake, breaking down barriers that have historically limited financial systems to a select few.

The benefits of DeFi are numerous. One of the most significant advantages is the reduction of transaction costs. By eliminating intermediaries, DeFi can offer services at a portion of the cost of traditional financial institutions, which often charge hefty fees. This cost efficiency is a game-changer, especially for developing regions with limited access to affordable financial services. Moreover, blockchain technology enables transparency in transactions, allowing them to be verified by anyone on the network. This transparency helps build countability among users and ensures all participants access the same information, reducing the potential for fraud and manipulation. For example, platforms like Uniswap and SushiSwap allow users to trade cryptocurrencies without having a centralized exchange, offering autonomy and control previously unavailable.

However, DeFi, like any transformative innovation, has its challenges. Security remains a significant concern. While smart contracts offer automation and trust, they are not infallible. Bugs in the code or vulnerabilities can lead to exploits, where malicious actors can drain funds from a contract. This risk emphasizes the need for rigorous code audits and security measures. Awareness of these challenges is the first step in navigating the DeFi landscape.

Additionally, DeFi's regulatory environment is still evolving. The need for clear regulations poses risks to users as governments worldwide grapple with how to oversee these decentralized systems. With proper frameworks, users may avoid legal uncertainties and potential losses if regulations shift unexpectedly.

Despite these challenges, DeFi's real-world applications are expanding rapidly. Lending and borrowing platforms like Aave and Compound gives users to earn interest on their crypto holdings or borrow against them without a credit check. This democratization of financial services opens doors for individuals otherwise excluded from traditional banking systems. As mentioned earlier, decentralized exchanges allow for the seamless trading of digital assets without centralized oversight, encouraging a more open market. These innovations illustrate the potential of DeFi to reshape the financial landscape, offering more inclusive, efficient, and transparent solutions. As we continue to explore the possibilities of DeFi, it's essential to weigh these benefits against the risks and challenges, understanding how each aspect fits into the broader narrative of financial evolution.

1.2 Altcoins Explained: Beyond Bitcoin

In the vast concept of cryptocurrencies, Bitcoin stands as the pioneering force. Yet, this is only the tip of the iceberg. Enter altcoins, a diverse array of digital currencies that serve as alternatives to Bitcoin. These altcoins are not mere imitators. They are innovators in their own right, introducing features and functionalities that address specific needs or inefficiencies in the crypto ecosystem. While Bitcoin was designed as a decentralized digital currency, altcoins expand on this concept by offering unique benefits and use cases. They include everything from payment systems to platforms for decentralized applications, and they each have their role to play in the evolving digital economy.

Take Ethereum, for instance. Known as the second largest cryptocurrency by market cap, Ethereum revolutionized the crypto space by introducing smart contracts and decentralized applications (dApps). Unlike Bitcoin, which focuses on peer-to-peer transactions, Ethereum provides a programmable blockchain for developers to build many applications. This flexibility has made Ethereum the backbone of decentralized finance and other blockchain-based projects. Then, there's Ripple (XRP), which targets the financial sector by offering fast and cost-effective cross-border payment solutions. Ripple's technology reduces transaction times from days to seconds, a significant leap forward for industries reliant on international money transfers.

Cardano brings something different, focusing on sustainability and proof-of-stake consensus. This approach enhances security and reduces the environmental impact associated with crypto mining. On the other hand, Chainlink addresses the need for reliable data feeds in smart contracts through its decentralized oracle networks. Chainlink has paved the way for more complex and valuable decentralized applications by enabling blockchains to interact with real-world data securely. These examples illustrate the breadth of innovation altcoins bring, each tackling a unique challenge or opening new possibilities within the blockchain space.

For investors, altcoins offer a valuable opportunity for portfolio diversification. As one wouldn't put all their eggs in a single basket, diversifying across different cryptocurrencies can spread risk and potentially increase returns. While Bitcoin remains a staple in many portfolios, altcoins can manifest in various sectors of the blockchain industry. However, it's essential to recognize the inherent volatility of altcoin markets. Prices can fluctuate dramatically, influenced by technological developments, market sentiment, and regulatory news. This volatility presents opportunities and risks, emphasizing the significance of thorough research and strategic planning in crypto investing.

Looking ahead, the future of altcoins seems promising. As blockchain technology evolves, we expect to see even more innovative uses for altcoins across various industries. The capable applications are vast and varied, from supply chain management to healthcare. Furthermore, integrating altcoins into everyday life could become more commonplace as more businesses and consumers adopt blockchain solutions. Technological advancements will also play a crucial role as scalability, security, and interoperability improvements drive the next wave of adoption. The altcoin market is not static; it is a dynamic and ever-evolving landscape that requires continuous learning and adaptation.

1.3 Stablecoins: The Bridge Between Crypto and Fiat

Stablecoins have emerged as a necessary component of the cryptocurrency ecosystem, bridging volatile digital assets and the relative stability of fiat currencies. These digital coins are pegged to traditional currencies like the U.S. dollar, providing stability that reduces the dramatic price swings often associated with other cryptocurrencies. By maintaining a consistent value, stablecoins offer a proven medium of exchange and a store of value, making them an attractive option for traders and investors looking to minimize risk. With their roots in the need for stability, stablecoins have become indispensable for seamlessly integrating crypto into everyday financial activities.

Their utility extends beyond the simple transaction. In trading, stablecoins offer a practical way to sidestep the volatility of traditional cryptocurrencies. Traders can quickly convert their assets into stablecoins to protect their portfolio's value during market downturns. This feature is crucial for those who wish to keep their assets within the crypto space without suffering losses due to sudden market shifts. Additionally, stablecoins serve as a stable store of value, providing a digital alternative to holding cash. This aspect benefits those who want digital assets but are wary of the unpredictability that usually accompanies them.

Stablecoins come in several forms, each maintaining its value through different mechanisms. Fiat-collateralized stablecoins are backed by reserves of traditional currencies, such as the U.S. dollar or the euro. This backing provides a tangible asset supporting the stablecoin's value, ensuring it can be redeemed at a fixed rate. On the other hand, crypto-collateralized stablecoins use reserves of other cryptocurrencies to maintain their stability. Though less common, they offer a decentralized alternative to fiat-backed options. Algorithmic stablecoins take a different approach, using algorithms to allocate the supply of coins based on demand, thereby maintaining their value. While innovative, these algorithmic models have experienced challenges in maintaining stability, as seen in past market events.

The practical applications of stablecoins are vast and varied. One significant use case is in the realm of international remittances. Traditional cross-border payments can be decelerating and costly, often taking several days to process and subjecting users to high fees. Stablecoins offer a faster, more cost-effective alternative, allowing users to transfer funds across borders in minutes. This capability is particularly beneficial for persons in developing countries who depend on remittances from family members abroad. In decentralized finance (DeFi), stablecoins play a crucial role by providing liquidity and mitigating volatility. They enable users to participate in lending, borrowing, and other financial activities without exposure to the price swings that characterize the broader crypto market.

However, stablecoins have their challenges. Regulatory scrutiny is a significant concern as governments and financial authorities worldwide deal with how to classify and oversee these digital assets. A comprehensive regulatory framework is necessary for issuers and users alike, potentially hindering the growth and adoption of stablecoins. In addition to regulatory issues, centralization is another consideration. Many stablecoins rely on centralized entities to manage reserves and maintain their value, which can introduce points of failure and counterparty risk. Addressing these challenges will enhance their reliability and foster user trust as the stablecoin market evolves.

As we conclude this exploration of stablecoins, it's clear that they are more than just a digital currency. They represent a crucial link between the traditional financial system and the burgeoning world of crypto, offering stability and utility in equal measure. Their ability to combine the best of both worlds makes them a linchpin in the future of finance. As you continue to explore the intricacies of digital currencies, remember that stablecoins stand as a testament to innovation in the pursuit of balance and accessibility in the financial landscape.

Chapter 2: Navigating the Crypto Ecosystem

Imagine walking into a vast digital marketplace bustling with activity and innovation. This marketplace isn't just a figment of the future—it's the present-day world of cryptocurrencies and digital assets. As you step into this space, you're immediately faced with myriad terms and concepts that can be daunting. Among these are "tokens" and "native tokens," two fundamental components that play distinct roles in the blockchain ecosystem. Knowing these elements is crucial for anyone looking to navigate the crypto landscape effectively, whether you're a young adult venturing into your first financial account, a seasoned investor, or an individual planning for retirement.

Tokens and native tokens differ primarily in their relationship to blockchain networks. Tokens are digital units created on top of existing blockchains like Ethereum. They serve various purposes, from granting access to services to representing assets. Native tokens, however, are integral to their respective blockchains, like Bitcoin or Ether; they are not just built on a blockchain; they are an essential part of it. This distinction is crucial because it influences how these assets function within their ecosystems. For instance, while Bitcoin operates as a standalone currency, tokens like DAI or LINK derive their utility from the Ethereum blockchain, which can be used in smart contracts or traded on decentralized platforms.

The applications for tokens are vast and varied, reflecting their versatile nature—utility tokens, for instance, grant holders access to a particular service or platform. Binance Coin (BNB), a utility token, allows users to remit transaction fees on the Binance exchange at a discounted rate, promoting its use within the trading community. Security tokens, on the other hand, represent ownership in an asset, much like traditional stocks. These tokens are often used in the tokenization of assets, where real-world items like real estate, art, or even intellectual property rights are represented by digital tokens. This representation makes them easier to trade and manage, as the tokens can be bought, sold, or traded on digital platforms, eliminating the need for physical transfer of the actual asset. This approach not only enhances liquidity but also democratizes access to investment opportunities, allowing more people, including you, to participate in markets that were previously out of reach, thereby empowering you as an investor.

Native tokens play a critical role in maintaining and securing their blockchain networks. They are the backbone of the blockchain, facilitating transactions and providing incentives for network participants. Bitcoin, for example, uses a consensus mechanism known as proof-of-work. In this mechanism, miners compete to solve complex mathematical puzzles, and the primary one to solve them gets to aggregate a new block of transactions to the blockchain and is rewarded with new bitcoins. This process ensures the integrity and security of the Bitcoin blockchain. Similarly, Ethereum uses Ether to pay for transaction fees and computational services on its network, enabling it to function as a global platform for decentralized applications. The importance of native tokens extends beyond their immediate utility. They are a driving force behind the security and efficiency of their respective blockchains, fostering an environment where innovation can thrive.

As you consider investing in cryptocurrencies, understanding the nuances between tokens and native tokens is vital. This knowledge can significantly influence your investment strategy, ensuring that you are well-informed and prepared. Diversification, for example, involves balancing your portfolio between utility tokens and native tokens to mitigate risk and capitalize on different growth opportunities. While utility tokens can offer high returns due to their specific use cases and potential for adoption, they also come with higher risks. On the other hand, native tokens, often more established, provide stability and are generally considered safer investments, giving you a sense of reassurance and confidence in your investment decisions.

Understanding the roles of tokens and native tokens opens up a world of possibilities within the crypto ecosystem. Whether you're looking to diversify your investments or simply want to grasp the intricacies of digital assets, this knowledge equips you with the tools to make informed decisions. As you explore these digital units' diverse applications and implications, you'll better appreciate their impact on the financial world. This understanding empowers you as an investor and ignites your excitement for the potential growth and innovation in the ever-evolving digital finance platform, fostering a sense of optimism about the future of cryptocurrencies.

2.2 NFTs Unveiled: More Than Digital Art

Non-fungible tokens, or NFTs, are unique in digital assets. Each NFT is distinct, unlike digital currencies such as Bitcoin or Ethereum, which can be exchanged one-to-one. This uniqueness is akin to owning an original painting or a rare collectible. No two NFTs are the same and cannot be divided into smaller units. This indivisibility is what distinguishes NFTs from other digital assets, and it is what gives them their intrinsic value. The NFT unit is a digital certificate of authenticity recorded on a blockchain, providing verifiable ownership and provenance. This feature is particularly appealing in a digital world where replication is easy and often rampant.

The potential of NFTs extends far beyond the digital art world, where they first gained prominence. In the gaming industry, for instance, NFTs are revolutionizing how players interact with virtual goods. Games like Axie Infinity allow players to own and trade in-game assets, such as characters and accessories, as NFTs. This ownership means players can buy, sell, or trade these assets outside the game, creating real-world value from virtual items. Similarly, in real estate, NFTs facilitate the tokenization of physical properties. This process involves creating digital tokens representing ownership stakes in a property, making buying and selling real estate more accessible and efficient. The music and entertainment industries also embrace NFTs to manage royalties and rights. Artists can use NFTs to sell their music directly to fans, ensuring they receive a fair share of the revenue while fans gain unique digital memorabilia.

The NFT market has witnessed remarkable growth, driven by increasing adoption and rising valuations. Initially, NFTs were primarily associated with digital art, but the market has expanded to include various industries. This growth is fueled by cross-industry collaborations, where traditional sectors partner with NFT platforms to create innovative solutions. For example, fashion brands explore NFTs for exclusive digital apparel, while sports franchises offer fans digital collectibles tied to their favorite teams. This convergence of traditional and digital realms opens new opportunities and challenges as businesses navigate the complexities of integrating NFTs into their existing models.

Despite their potential, NFTs have challenges and criticisms. The environmental impact of blockchain networks minting and trading NFTs is a primary concern. The energy consumption associated with these processes has drawn significant scrutiny, prompting calls for more sustainable practices. Some blockchain platforms are already transitioning to less energy-intensive consensus mechanisms, but the issue remains a contention. The NFT market is also susceptible to speculation, with prices sometimes soaring to unsustainable levels. This volatility can lead to sudden market corrections, posing risks for investors who need more preparation for such fluctuations. Critics argue that the hype surrounding NFTs has created a bubble that could burst, leaving many with devalued assets.

In the digital age, NFTs reshape how we think about ownership and value. They offer a new level of engagement, allowing investors to own a piece of the digital world tangibly. As you explore the potential of NFTs, consider the diverse applications and the evolving landscape. Whether you are interested in gaming, real estate, music, or beyond, NFTs present opportunities to participate in a dynamic and innovative market; however, it's essential to remain perceptive of the challenges and criticisms accompanying this burgeoning field as the technology and market continue to develop.

Web3: The New Internet Paradigm

Web3 marks a revolutionary shift in how we perceive and interact with the internet. At its core, Web3 represents a departure from the traditional, centralized Internet model, promising a decentralized digital landscape where user control is distributed rather than concentrated in the hands of a few corporations. This transition is driven by two fundamental principles: decentralization and user ownership. In the Web3 world, decentralization means that any single entity does not control data and transactions. Instead, they are managed by a network of users, each with a say in how the system operates. This shift empowers individuals, giving them more control over their digital lives. User ownership, another cornerstone of Web3, allows individuals to own and manage their data, ensuring privacy and autonomy in an increasingly connected world.

The technologies that underpin Web3 are both innovative and transformative. Blockchain technology is the foundation, providing the infrastructure for a decentralized internet. It enables the creation of decentralized applications, or dApps, which operate independently of central servers. These applications, such as Uniswap for decentralized finance and OpenSea for NFT trading, previously only offered possible services through centralized entities. The technology behind these dApps is designed to be transparent and permissionless, allowing anyone to participate without intermediaries. Interoperability is another key aspect of Web3. It pertains to the ability of different blockchain networks to communicate and interact with one another, facilitating a seamless exchange of data and value across platforms. This capability is necessary for the growth and efficiency of the Web3 ecosystem, enabling diverse applications to work together in harmony.

Web3's impact on society and everyday life is profound and far-reaching. By enhancing privacy and security, Web3 offers a level of data protection that was previously unattainable. Users can control their personal information, deciding who can access it and how it is used. This control reduces the risk of data breaches and unauthorized use, fostering a digital environment prioritizing user safety. In addition to privacy, Web3 introduces new economic models that redefine value creation and distribution. These models are built on decentralization and user empowerment, allowing individuals to earn and trade value directly without intermediaries. This shift democratizes access to economic opportunities, enabling more people to participate in and benefit from the digital economy.

Despite its potential, Web3 faces significant challenges that must be addressed for widespread adoption. Usability remains a significant barrier, as many current platforms are complex and challenging for the average user to navigate. Simplifying these platforms is crucial to making Web3 accessible to a broader audience. Scalability is another critical issue. As more users and applications join the Web3 ecosystem, the technology must handle increased demand without compromising performance. Developing scalable solutions will be essential to accommodate this growth and ensure that Web3 can support a global user base.

As we conclude this exploration of Web3, it's clear that this new internet paradigm has the potential to reshape our digital landscape in profound ways. By empowering individuals and fostering a more open and inclusive internet, Web3 offers exciting possibilities for innovation and collaboration. As we move forward, addressing the challenges of usability and scalability will be key to realizing the full potential of this transformative technology. The next chapter will explore practical aspects of cryptocurrency trading, offering insights and strategies to navigate this dynamic market confidently.

Chapter 3: Trading Strategies for All Levels

Picture yourself in a bustling marketplace, around traders swiftly exchanging goods. Some are seasoned veterans, while others are eager newcomers. The world of cryptocurrency trading mirrors this vibrant scene, brimming with opportunities but also fraught with risks. As you enter this dynamic environment, you must arm yourself with strategies aligning with your goals and risk tolerance. This chapter delves into conservative trading approaches, which are fitting for those who prioritize capital preservation while navigating the potential of the crypto market.

In conservative trading, one of the most effective techniques is dollar-cost averaging (DCA). This strategy involves regularly investing a fixed sum of money into cryptocurrencies, regardless of market conditions. By doing so, you smooth out the highs and lows of market fluctuations, buying more when prices are low and less when they are high; this approach lessens the impact of volatility and instills discipline in your investment habits, preventing emotional decisions based on short-term market movements.

Over time, DCA can lead to a favorable average purchase price, minimizing the risks associated with lump-sum investments.

Diversification is a key pillar of conservative trading, offering a sense of control in the unpredictable cryptocurrency market. This concept, akin to the age-old precept of not putting all your eggs in one basket, involves spreading your investments across various assets. In the cryptocurrency world, diversification could signify investing in a mix of Bitcoin, Ethereum, and carefully selected altcoins, each with different risk profiles and growth potentials. This strategy is a cushion for your portfolio during market downturns, as the performance of one asset can offset the underperformance of another. While diversification doesn't eliminate risk, it does mitigate it, offering a more balanced approach to investing and a sense of security in the face of market volatility.

When considering which cryptocurrencies to include in your conservative portfolio, focus on stable asset investments. Bitcoin and Ethereum, often blue-chip cryptocurrencies, are well-established and widely recognized. Their resilience and substantial market capitalization make them less volatile than newer, less tested coins. Incorporating stablecoins like USDC (USD Coin) or USDT (Tether) can also provide a hedge against market volatility. These digital assets are pegged to traditional currencies, offering stability in market turbulence. By including stablecoins in your portfolio, you can hold onto gains without exiting the crypto market entirely, maintaining liquidity for future opportunities.

Technical analysis is essential for conservative traders seeking to identify low-risk entry points. This method involves evaluating historical price data and using patterns to forecast future movements. A fundamental concept in technical analysis is support and resistance levels. These are price points where a cryptocurrency tends to stop and reverse its direction. For instance, a support level is a price at which a cryptocurrency's tendencies fall and start rising, while a resistance level is a price at which a cryptocurrency aims to stop growing and start falling. Recognizing these levels can help you decide when to buy or sell. Another valuable tool is moving averages, which are calculated by aggregating the closing prices of a cryptocurrency over a certain number of days and then dividing by the number of days. This smooths out price data to highlight trends over time. By understanding these patterns, you can identify optimal times to enter or exit trades, minimizing risk while maximizing potential returns.

Appointing realistic expectations is a cornerstone of a sustainable trading strategy. It's vital to remember that cryptocurrencies are inherently volatile. While they offer significant growth potential, they also carry risks. Long-term holding is a strategy that underscores patience and the belief in gradual growth. Maintaining a long-term perspective, you can weather short-term fluctuations and focus on the broader trajectory of your investments. Additionally, it's prudent to steer clear of high leverage, which can amplify gains and losses. Avoiding excessive leverage safeguards your capital from rapid swings that can lead to substantial losses.

Reflection Section: Evaluating Personal Risk Tolerance

Take a moment to reflect on your risk tolerance. How comfortable are you with market volatility? Consider your financial goals and the time horizon for your investments. Please write down your thoughts and use them to guide your trading strategy, ensuring that it aligns with your personal comfort level and financial objectives.

3.2 Aggressive Trading Techniques: Maximizing Gains

Imagine standing on the edge of a fast-moving river, looking for the perfect spot to jump in and ride the current. This image captures the essence of aggressive trading, which aims to capitalize on high-volatility opportunities and the potential for exciting high returns. While demanding quick thinking and a solid understanding of market dynamics, this approach also holds the potential for exciting high returns. Day trading, a popular strategy, includes making several trades within a given day to exploit short-term price movements. The key here is speed and precision. Successful day traders have a keen eye for patterns and trends, allowing them to enter and exit positions at just the right moments. They rely heavily on real-time data and technical indicators to guide their decisions.

Swing trading, nevertheless, takes a slightly longer view. Instead of focusing on minute-by-minute fluctuations, swing traders hold positions for multiple days or weeks to profit from expected price swings. This strategy suits those who prefer a more measured approach while still seeking to benefit from market volatility. Swing trading involves analyzing medium-term trends and identifying potential reversal points. It's about patience and timing, waiting for the opportune moment to make a move. Both day and swing trading require discipline, a well-thought-out plan, and the ability to act decisively under pressure. This patience in waiting for the right moment can make you feel calm and collected in the face of market volatility.

Leverage is another tool in the aggressive trader's arsenal. By borrowing funds to increase the size of a trade, traders can amplify potential returns. However, with great power comes great responsibility, and leverage is no exception. While it can magnify profits, it can equally amplify losses, making risk management crucial. Margin trading allows traders to borrow money against their existing holdings to increase their buying power; this can be particularly advantageous in a climbing market, but it's important to set strict stop-loss orders to limit potential losses. Stop-loss orders automatically sell a position if it reaches a specific price, safeguarding your portfolio from unexpected downturns.

Advanced technical analysis tools are indispensable for maximizing gains through aggressive trading. One such tool is Fibonacci retracement, which uses key ratios to identify potential reversal levels. These levels can serve as valuable indicators of where a price might pull back before continuing in its original direction. For instance, the most common Fibonacci retracement levels are 23.6%, 38.2%, 50%, 61.8%, and 100%. Another helpful tool is Bollinger Bands, which helps analyze volatility and relative price levels. They visually represent how prices deviate from their average, assisting traders to anticipate potential breakouts or breakdowns. Mastery of these tools enables traders to make more informed decisions, improving their chances of successful trades.

Arbitrage opportunities present another avenue for profit in the aggressive trading landscape. This strategy involves exploiting price differences across different markets or exchanges. Cross-exchange arbitrage, for instance, takes advantage of discrepancies in the price of a cryptocurrency on two separate exchanges. Traders can profit by trading on the less expensive exchange and selling on the more expensive one. Triangular arbitrage denotes taking advantage of price differences between three different cryptocurrencies. This method requires quick action and a keen understanding of market dynamics, as these opportunities can disappear in seconds.

Aggressive trading is not for the faint of heart. It requires combining technical knowledge, strategic planning, and a willingness to take calculated risks. Traders can maximize their potential gains by recognizing high-volatility opportunities, utilizing leverage responsibly, applying advanced technical analysis, and exploring arbitrage. This approach demands focus and dedication, but the recompense can be substantial for those willing to embrace the challenge.

3.3 Balancing Act: When to Switch Strategies

Knowing when to shift gears between conservative and aggressive strategies can be pivotal in cryptocurrency trading. Market conditions play an essential role in this decision-making process. Recognizing whether we're in a bull or bear market can help inform your approach. In a bull market, prices rise, and optimism reigns. This environment might encourage a more aggressive stance to capitalize on upward trends.

Conversely, where prices decline, a bear market often calls for a more conservative approach to protecting your assets. Understanding the broader economic indicators, such as interest rates, inflation, and geopolitical events, also provides valuable context. These factors can influence market sentiment and help you decide whether a pivot in your strategy is necessary.

Your personal risk tolerance is another significant factor in determining when to switch strategies. Each individual's financial situation is unique, shaped by income, expenses, and long-term goals. Assessing your financial stability involves taking stock of your current assets, liabilities, and investment objectives. Are you investing for retirement or looking to make a quick profit? This clarity will guide your trading decisions. Equally important is your emotional resilience. The crypto market is notoriously volatile, and getting trapped in the emotional highs and lows is easy. Understanding how you react to market fluctuations will guide you in avoiding impulsive decisions that may not align with your long-term strategy.

Flexibility in your trading plan is key to adapting to changing circumstances. A dynamic allocation strategy allows you to shift your asset allocation based on market outlooks. For instance, if the market shows signs of recovery, you might increase your exposure to higher-risk assets. Conversely, in uncertain times, you might pivot towards more stable investments. Regularly rebalancing your portfolio is also vital. This process involves adjusting your holdings to maintain your desired risk level, ensuring your portfolio remains aligned with your financial goals. Rebalancing helps you capitalize on gains and protect against losses, maintaining a steady course through market turbulence.

Continuous evaluation of your trading performance is essential for refining your strategies. Overseeing performance metrics such as return on investment (ROI) and win-loss ratios provides insight into how well your plan works. This data lets you make informed adjustments, optimizing your approach over time. Reflecting on past trades is also a valuable exercise. Analyzing what went right or wrong helps identify areas for improvement, turning mistakes into learning opportunities. This iterative process is crucial for developing a robust trading strategy that evolves with the market and your personal growth as an investor.

As you balance conservative and aggressive trading, understand that flexibility and adaptability are essential allies. Switching strategies based on market conditions, personal risk tolerance, and performance evaluation is a skill honed over time. This balancing act requires discipline and openness to change, ensuring your trading approach remains resilient in an ever-changing market landscape. As we conclude this chapter on trading strategies, we've explored the intricacies of managing risk, maximizing gains, and adapting to market dynamics. Each strategy serves a purpose, offering tools to navigate the crypto market's complexity. With a solid foundation in these techniques, you are better equipped to face the challenges and opportunities that lie ahead. The next chapter will explore the essential tools and resources to enhance your trading experience, providing the means to refine further and execute your strategies effectively.

Chapter 4: Building a Secure Foundation

Imagine the digital marketplace as a bustling bazaar filled with countless stalls, each claiming to offer the best wares. In this vibrant environment, choosing the right stall—or, in our case, the proper cryptocurrency exchange—becomes vital. This choice isn't just about convenience; it's about placing the groundwork for a secure and profitable trading experience. Selecting an exchange is akin to picking a financial partner. It necessitates careful consideration of several factors that ensure your assets remain safe and accessible. This chapter will examine the essential elements that make an exchange trustworthy and efficient, equipping you with the knowledge to make informed decisions.

4.1 Choosing the Right Exchange: What to Look For

When selecting an exchange, the digital marketplace is a place of both opportunities and risks. Security features need to be at the top of your priority list. (2-FA)Two-factor authentication is a critical security measure that adds an extra layer of protection. It requires a second verification form in addition to your password, such as a code transmitted to your cellphone or email. This step significantly reduces the likelihood of unauthorized access, ensuring that even if someone guesses your password, they can't proceed without the secondary code. Another key feature is cold storage, where exchanges keep most of their funds offline. This practice protects against hacking attempts, as offline assets are less vulnerable to cyber threats. Some exchanges even offer insurance policies to cover potential losses from unforeseen events. These policies provide an added layer of security, offering peace of mind that your investments are protected.

User experience is another critical consideration. An intuitive interface matters greatly, especially for those new to crypto. Seek platforms that offer seamless navigation and clear instructions. This ease of use should extend to all users, from beginners taking their first steps to experienced traders executing complex strategies. Additionally, responsive customer support is vital. In the fast-paced world of crypto, timely assistance can help resolve issues quickly, preventing potential losses. Whether through live chat, email, or cellphone, ensure that the exchange offers multiple avenues for support.

Regulatory compliance is not merely a legal requisite; it's a safeguard for your investments. Exchanges must adhere to licensing requirements set by financial authorities, ensuring they operate within legal boundaries. This compliance provides oversight that can protect you from fraudulent activity, giving you a sense of security and peace of mind. Understanding and being aware of these regulations can empower you, as it ensures you deal with a legitimate and accountable entity.

Fees and trading options are also significant considerations. Each exchange has its fee structure, which can impact your profitability. Understanding these costs can help you select an exchange that pairs with your budget and trading style. This understanding can make you feel more financially savvy and in control of your investments. Moreover, it examines the range of supported cryptocurrencies. An exchange offering various trading pairs provides flexibility, allowing you to diversify your portfolio without switching platforms frequently. This diversity can be a boon for traders exploring different market opportunities.

Exercise: Exchange Evaluation Checklist

- Security Features: Does the exchange offer 2FA, cold storage, and insurance policies?

- For instance, Binance offers 2FA, cold storage, and insurance policies, making it a secure choice. User Experience: Is the platform easy for beginners and experienced traders to navigate? Is customer support responsive? Coinbase is a prime example of a platform that excels in user experience with its intuitive interface and responsive customer support. Regulatory Compliance: Is the exchange licensed and compliant with KYC/AML protocols?

- Fees and Trading Options: Are the transaction fees competitive? Does the exchange support a wide range of cryptocurrencies?

Using this checklist, you can systematically evaluate potential exchanges, ensuring you choose a platform that meets your security, usability, and trading needs. Considering these factors, remember that a secure foundation is key to a successful crypto trading experience.

4.2 Top Exchanges for Secure Trading: A Curated List

Navigating the world of cryptocurrency exchanges can feel like standing in front of an endless buffet. Each option promises the best flavors, but only a few truly deliver on their promises of security and reliability. Among these, Binance stands out for its comprehensive suite of offerings. With a vast array of cryptocurrencies available, it caters to both the casual trader and the seasoned investor. Binance doesn't stop at trading; it expands into decentralized applications through its Binance Smart Chain, a feature that has attracted developers and investors alike. This ecosystem fosters innovation by allowing users to create and participate in decentralized applications, broadening the scope of what can be achieved with blockchain technology.

Coinbase, another heavyweight in the exchange arena, is renowned for its user-friendly design, making it an ideal starting point for beginners. Its interface is intuitive, requiring minimal effort to navigate, reducing intimidation for those new to cryptocurrency. Beyond ease of use, Coinbase provides necessary security options, including insurance coverage for digital assets stored on its platform. This extra layer of protection is comforting, offering a safety net against potential breaches. For more experienced users, Coinbase Pro offers advanced trading features, such as real-time order books and charting tools, allowing for more sophisticated trading strategies. The convenience of a user-friendly platform like Coinbase can make your trading experience more comfortable and less daunting.

Kraken, known for its stringent regulatory compliance, has carved a niche by prioritizing security and transparency. Its adherence to regulations instills confidence in users, reassuring them that their investments are in safe hands. Kraken also stands out with its advanced security measures, including a high percentage of assets held in cold storage. This practice minimizes online vulnerabilities, safeguarding user funds. Furthermore, Kraken's strong regulatory framework has earned it a reputation for reliability, making it a preferred choice for those prioritizing security and compliance.

User feedback can be a goldmine of information when choosing an exchange. Analyzing platforms like Trustpilot gives you a snapshot of real user experiences and satisfaction levels. Positive reviews often highlight ease of use, responsive customer service, and reliable security measures. Conversely, negative reviews may flag issues such as slow withdrawal processes or high fees. Social media sentiment also plays a critical role in gauging an exchange's reputation. Platforms like Twitter and Reddit host vibrant communities where users share their experiences and opinions, providing a grassroots-level perspective on an exchange's performance and trustworthiness. Leveraging user feedback can provide reassurance and a sense of security in your trading journey.

Staying updated on the latest developments in the crypto exchange landscape is vital. How an exchange responds to security breaches reveals much about its integrity and commitment to safeguarding user assets. For instance, Binance faced a significant security breach in 2019 but responded swiftly, compensating affected users and enhancing its security protocols. Such actions demonstrate an exchange's resilience and dedication to maintaining trust. Additionally, keeping abreast of new features and tools exchanges offer can enhance your trading experience. For example, Coinbase's introduction of staking services allows users to gain rewards by holding specific cryptocurrencies, adding a new dimension to asset management.

In the ever-evolving world of cryptocurrency, selecting the proper exchange is more than a choice—it's a strategic measure that can significantly impact your trading success and security. Each platform offers unique strengths and caters to different trading needs, whether you're drawn to

Binance's extensive crypto selection, Coinbase's user-friendly approach, or Kraken's robust compliance and security. The key lies in understanding your trading goals and aligning them with the features and reputation of the exchange you choose.

4.3 Safeguarding Your Assets: Security Measures for Peace of Mind

In cryptocurrency's vast and often unpredictable world, safeguarding your assets is paramount. One of the most straightforward yet effective strategies is implementing strong password practices. The digital realm demands more than just the password you use for your social media accounts. Here, complexity is your ally. A strong password should mix uppercase and lowercase letters, numbers, and symbols. It should be unique for each account you hold. This practice minimizes the risk that a breach on one platform could compromise your digital presence. To manage these complex passwords, consider using a password manager. These tools generate robust passwords and store them securely, sparing you the hassle of remembering each one. Additionally, update your passwords regularly. This simple act can significantly lessen the risk of unauthorized access, keeping your accounts secure.

Another pivotal step in securing your cryptocurrency is the use of hardware wallets. Contrary to software wallets, which are connected to the internet and therefore vulnerable to online threats, hardware wallets store your private keys offline. This offline storage method drastically reduces the likelihood of cyberattacks, providing a fortress-like level of security for your digital assets. Popular hardware wallets like Ledger and Trezor have built their reputations on reliability and security, offering peace of mind that your investments are shielded from digital theft. With a hardware wallet, you maintain complete control over your cryptocurrencies, away from the prying eyes of hackers. This level of security is especially crucial for long-term storage and significant holdings, where the stakes are higher.

Phishing scams pose another threat in the crypto space. These scams are designed to deceive you into revealing sensitive information under the guise of legitimate communications. Often, these attacks start with emails or SMS messages that mimic and con trusted sources, urging you to click on links that lead to counterfeit websites. Recognizing these fraudulent communications is vital. Be cautious of emails with poor grammar, odd sender addresses, or urgent calls to action. Constantly verify the authenticity of a website before entering any personal information. Never click on suspicious links, and never download attachments from phishing sources. By staying vigilant against phishing attempts, you secure yourself from inevitable financial losses and identity theft.

Monitoring your account activity is another layer of protection that should be noticed. Setting up alerts for unusual transactions can act as an early warning system, notifying you immediately if there is any unauthorized access. These alerts can be suited to your preferences, such as large withdrawals or transactions from unfamiliar locations. Regularly reviewing your transaction history is equally important. By keeping a close eye on your account activity, you can quickly spot discrepancies and take prompt action to rectify any issues. Being proactive ensures you remain in control of your assets, minimizing the risk of unauthorized transactions.

Security in the crypto world is about building a robust defense system that protects your assets from various threats. Implementing strong password practices, utilizing hardware wallets, staying aware of phishing scams, and monitoring account activity are critical components of this defense. As you fortify your security measures, remember that these practices not only protect your current investments but also pave the way for a more secure and confident trading experience in the future. In the next chapter, we'll explore the intricacies of digital wallets, delving into their functionalities and how they can further enhance your security and trading efficiency, which will provide you with the utilities needed to manage your digital assets effectively, ensuring you are better prepared for the challenges and opportunities in cryptocurrency.

Chapter 5: Mastering Digital Wallets

In the vast ocean of cryptocurrency, digital wallets are your sturdy vessel, guiding you through the waves of transactions, storage, and security. Unlike the physical wallets we carry in our pockets, these digital counterparts are gateways to crypto, enabling you to manage your digital assets quickly and precisely. MetaMask is one of the most widely used digital wallets, renowned for its versatility and robust features. It is a secure vault for Ether and other Ethereum-based tokens and a bridge to many decentralized applications. Today, with over 30 million users globally, MetaMask integrates an essential tool for anyone venturing into the digital currency space, offering both browser extensions and mobile app versions.

5.1 Setting Up Your MetaMask: A Step-by-Step Guide

To harness the power of MetaMask, you first need to set it up on your preferred platform. MetaMask is available as a browser extension for Chrome and

Firefox if you use a desktop or laptop. Begin by visiting the official MetaMask website or your browser's extension store. Once there, download and install the extension. It's crucial to ensure you're downloading from a legitimate source to avoid potential security risks. After installation, the MetaMask icon will appear in your browser toolbar, signaling that you're ready to proceed. For anyone who prefers to manage their digital assets on the go, MetaMask offers an app compatible with both iOS and Android devices. Go to your device's app store, search for MetaMask, and download the app. Once installed, open MetaMask and initiate the setup process, which mirrors the browser extension setup in simplicity and security.

Creating and securing your wallet is the next critical step. Upon launching MetaMask, you will be prompted to create a new wallet. This process involves setting a strong password as your first defense against unauthorized access. A well-crafted password combines uppercase and lowercase letters, numbers, and symbols to enhance security. Equally important is the seed phrase, also known as the Secret Recovery Phrase. This series of 12 words is your lifeline in case you need to recover your wallet. It's crucial to understand that this phrase is not just a backup but the only way to regain access to your assets if your device is lost or compromised. Store this phrase in a secure, offline location—never digitally or online—to prevent unauthorized access. It's your ultimate safeguard, ensuring you retain access to your digital assets even if your device is lost or compromised.

Configuring network settings is where you tailor MetaMask to suit your specific needs. By default, MetaMask connects to the Ethereum mainnet, the primary network for Ethereum transactions. However, switch to testnets for experimentation or add custom networks for decentralized finance applications. To switch networks, open MetaMask, click on the network dropdown menu, and select your desired network. For custom networks, go to the custom RPC settings and input the necessary details to connect. These configurations allow you to explore various blockchain networks, expanding your reach in the crypto ecosystem.

Using MetaMask for transactions is where its functionality truly shines. Click the 'Send' button within the MetaMask interface to send tokens. Enter the recipient's wallet address, specify the amount, and choose your preferred transaction fee. It's important to note that the transaction fee, also known as the 'gas fee, 'is the amount you pay miners to process your transaction on the blockchain.

MetaMask will calculate the gas fee needed to process the transaction, providing an estimate based on current network conditions. After reviewing the details, confirm the transaction to initiate the transfer. Receiving tokens is equally straightforward; click on your account name to copy your wallet address and share it with the sender. Once the transaction is confirmed on the blockchain, the tokens will arrive in your MetaMask wallet.

Practical Exercise: MetaMask Mastery

Take a moment to familiarize yourself with the MetaMask and Trust Wallet interfaces. Explore the various settings, including network options and security features. Practice sending a small amount of cryptocurrency to a friend or another wallet you own. Note the transaction details and fees involved. These wallets are designed with user affability in mind, making navigating and understanding their capabilities and functionalities easy. By the end of this exercise, you should be able to easily navigate the MetaMask and Trust Wallet interfaces, understand the different network options, and be confident in conducting transactions with them.

5.2 Navigating Trust Wallet: Features and Security

Trust Wallet is a mighty digital wallet and comprehensive hub for managing many cryptocurrencies. With its support for over 250,000 different cryptocurrencies and tokens across over 65 blockchains, it offers unprecedented flexibility. This multi-currency system means you can control all your digital assets in one place, eliminating the hassle of dealing with multiple wallets. Trust Wallet simplifies the tracking and tracing of your investments, making it easier to see the big picture. But its capabilities continue. Trust Wallet also features a built-in DApp browser, which allows you to access decentralized applications seamlessly. This feature opens the door to a world of decentralized finance (DeFi) projects, enabling you to interact with the blockchain directly from your wallet without navigating to another platform.

Downloading and configuring Trust Wallet on your mobile device is a straightforward process. Start by downloading the app from your device's official app store to ensure you get the legitimate version free from tampering. When installed, open the application and follow the prompts to create a new wallet. You'll need to generate a secure password and store your recovery phrase—a critical series of 12 words that act as your backup. This phrase is your lifeline. If you ever lose access to your wallet, write it down and keep it in a safe place. Trust Wallet can also import existing wallets using recovery phrases if you migrate from another wallet. This feature makes transitioning smooth, letting you consolidate your digital assets without losing your transaction history or funds.

Trust Wallet is committed to protecting your digital assets with state-of-the-art security measures. One of its standout features is biometric authentication, which allows you to unlock your wallet using your fingerprint or facial recognition. An added layer of security ensures that only you can access your funds. Trust Wallet also prioritizes backup and recovery options to protect against loss. By enabling automatic backups and securely storing your recovery phrase, you can ensure access to your assets under any circumstances. These measures reflect Trust Wallet's dedication to providing a secure environment for your digital investments, giving you peace of mind as you navigate the world of cryptocurrencies.

Transacting with Trust Wallet is both secure and efficient. To send cryptocurrencies, select the asset you wish to transfer, enter the recipient's wallet address, and specify the amount. The app will calculate the necessary transaction fee based on network conditions, ensuring your transaction is processed smoothly. Once confirmed, your transaction will be securely broadcasted to the blockchain. Trust Wallet also offers staking options, allowing you to earn passive income from your holdings. By participating in staking, you can support blockchain networks while earning rewards, adding another dimension to your investment strategy. This feature is integrated directly into the app, making it easy to manage and track your staking activities alongside your other assets.

Trust Wallet's user-friendly interface and comprehensive security features provide an excellent choice for managing digital assets. Whether sending cryptocurrencies or exploring staking opportunities, Trust Wallet delivers the tools to navigate the crypto landscape confidently.

5.3 Wallet Security Best Practices: Protecting Your Investments

Cryptocurrency offers incredible opportunities, but with these comes the critical responsibility of securing your digital assets. The digital wallet is your fortress; its security cannot be overstated. Understanding potential security risks is paramount when transactions are irreversible and digital theft is a real threat. It's essential to cultivate a security mindset that treats vigilance as a daily habit. This means knowing the threats, from phishing attacks that steal your login credentials to malware designed to capture your keystrokes. By recognizing these dangers, you can proactively protect your investments.

Implementing multi-layered security is a smart strategy for safeguarding your digital wallet. Two-factor authentication (2FA) is a crucial measure that increases the security of your accounts by providing an extra layer of protection. It requires a password and a second verification form, like a text message code or an authenticator app. This drastically reduces the chance of unauthorized access. Alongside 2FA, integrating a hardware wallet can bolster your security setup. Cold hardware wallets store your private keys offline, providing safety and security from online hacks. Using a hardware wallet effectively adds a physical barrier that hackers cannot penetrate from the internet.

Educating yourself about common security threats enhances your ability to avoid them. Phishing attacks are notoriously deceptive, often masquerading as legitimate emails or websites to con you into revealing sensitive information. Always double-check the sender's address and the URL of any website you visit. If something seems off, it probably is. Malware and keyloggers are other threats to be wary of. These malicious programs can infiltrate your devices through seemingly harmless downloads or email attachments. Keeping your antivirus software up-to-date is critical; it acts as a shield, detecting and neutralizing these threats before they can cause harm.

Regular maintenance of your digital wallet and devices is another pillar of security. Ensuring your wallet software is updated means the latest security patches protect you. Developers regularly release updates to address vulnerabilities, so make it a habit to install these as soon as they're available. Similarly, routine security checks should be part of your regular practice. Review your security settings, make sure your recovery phrases are stored safely, and double-check that your backup processes are in place. Doing so ensures that your security measures remain robust and up-to-date.

In digital finance, security isn't just an option—it's a necessity. Understanding the risks and taking precautions protects your digital assets from potential threats. This proactive approach safeguards your investments and allows you to engage with cryptocurrencies with confidence and peace of mind. As we conclude this chapter, remember that a secure wallet is your best defense against the unpredictable nature of the crypto market. The next chapter will explore leveraging your crypto holdings through strategies like staking and opening new avenues for passive income and financial growth.

Chapter 6: Staking and Passive Income

Chapter 6: Staking and Passive Income. Staking, a revolutionary concept in cryptocurrency, offers a unique opportunity for your money to work for you, even while you sleep. This innovative strategy, often hailed as a way to earn passive income, allows you to participate actively in the blockchain ecosystem. Unlike traditional savings accounts with minimal interest rates, staking enables you to earn rewards by locking up your digital assets, thereby supporting the network's security and operations. This process is a win-win for both the participant and the blockchain, making it a compelling strategy for novice and experienced investors. The potential for significant passive income, which can be a source of excitement and motivation, makes staking an exciting prospect for those interested in cryptocurrency investment.

To understand staking, let's first delve into the Proof-of-Stake (PoS) model, a consensus mechanism that underpins many modern blockchains. Unlike Proof of Work (PoW), which requires solving complex puzzles with high energy consumption, PoS relies on validators selected based on the number of coins they hold and willing to 'stake' as collateral. This approach reduces the need for extensive computational power, making it more environmentally friendly and accessible to a broader audience. Validator nodes play a crucial role in this process. They validate transactions and integrate new blocks into the blockchain. If a node acts maliciously or fails to validate correctly, it risks losing a portion of its staked assets—a process known as slashing. Slashing is a penalty mechanism to discourage dishonest behavior and ensure the network's security. This mechanism ensures that validators maintain the network's integrity, aligning their interests with the system's security and efficiency.

Staking offers several compelling benefits that appeal to both novice and experienced investors. First, it provides regular rewards, effectively earning interest on your staked assets. These rewards, often called 'staking rewards, 'come as newly minted tokens or a share of transaction fees, offering a consistent income stream without the necessity for active trading. This feature makes staking an attractive option for those seeking to grow their crypto holdings passively. By staking your assets, you also play a crucial role in the network's security and stability. Your participation helps secure the blockchain against attacks, promoting decentralization and enhancing the system's overall resilience. This staking aspect empowers you to support the technologies you believe in, making you an integral part of the crypto ecosystem.

However, staking has its risks and requirements. One of the primary considerations is the lock-up period, during which your assets are immobilized and cannot be traded. This lack of liquidity means you cannot access your funds quickly in response to market changes, such as sudden price spikes or crashes, potentially limiting your ability to react to these opportunities or downturns. Additionally, slashing risks threaten your staked assets, as validators can face penalties for misbehavior or downtime. Understanding these risks and selecting reputable validators is crucial to minimize potential losses.

Moreover, participating in staking requires a defined level of technical understanding and knowledge of the specific blockchain protocol. Though many platforms have simplified the process, a basic grasp of the mechanics is essential for effective participation. This emphasis on understanding the process will make you feel informed and prepared for your staking journey and empower you with confidence and control over your investments.

Several platforms offer staking opportunities, each catering to different preferences and levels of expertise. Centralized exchanges like Binance and Kraken provide user-friendly interfaces, making it easy for beginners to stake their assets with minimal effort. However, conducting thorough research and choosing a platform that coincides with your goals and risk tolerance are essential. Decentralized solutions like Lido and Rocket Pool offer alternatives that align with the decentralized finance ethos, often providing better yields due to lower overheads. Platforms like Tezos, Cosmos, and Algorand offer staking rewards at various rates. Careful selection is key to a successful staking experience, and it will provide you with a sense of security and reassurance in your investment decisions.

Reflection Section: Staking Readiness Checklist

- Understand the Proof-of-Stake mechanism and how it differs from Proof-of-Work.

- Evaluate your risk tolerance and the implications of lock-up periods.

- Research and select a reputable validator or platform for staking.

- Ensure you have the technical knowledge to participate effectively.

Incorporating these considerations into your staking strategy can help maximize your passive income potential while minimizing risks. This approach empowers you to confidently engage with the crypto ecosystem, leveraging your assets to earn rewards while contributing to the network's security and vitality.

6.2 Staking Different Cryptocurrencies: A Comparative Guide

As you explore the staking world, you must recognize that not all cryptocurrencies offer the same opportunities. Each has its unique staking features and potential rewards. Ethereum 2.0 is a notable example, significantly shifting from its previous model to a proof-of-stake system. This transition reduces energy consumption and enhances network security and scalability. When you stake Ethereum, you support this groundbreaking evolution while earning rewards. The participation requirements are relatively high, as you need to hold at least 32 ETH to run your validator node. However, many platforms offer pooled staking options, allowing you to join forces with other users to meet the minimum requirement.

Cardano offers another compelling staking opportunity. This platform allows you to delegate your ADA tokens to a stake pool. Delegated staking is a process where you assign your staking rights to a third party, usually a stake pool operator, who then includes your stake in their pool's total stake. This process, known as 'delegated staking, 'is user-friendly and doesn't require you to lock your tokens, providing flexibility while earning rewards. But what's truly unique about Cardano's approach is the emphasis on community involvement. Delegating ADA gives you a say in network decisions, making you an active participant in the blockchain's governance. This model fosters a strong, collaborative ecosystem where your voice matters. The entry barrier is low, making it accessible to a broad audience, and the returns are competitive, attracting both small and large investors alike.

Polkadot introduces a unique twist to staking with its nomination system. As a DOT holder, you can nominate validators who secure the network and process transactions. This system incentivizes active participation, as the choice of validators directly impacts your staking rewards. Polkadot's staking mechanism balances decentralization with efficiency, ensuring the network remains secure and robust. The minimum staking amount varies, but the community-driven approach allows you to incorporate it with the network's development. The potential returns from staking DOT are attractive, reflecting the network's innovative design and growth potential.

When evaluating staking yields and returns, it's crucial to understand that these can vary significantly across different cryptocurrencies. The Annual Percentage Yield (APY) you can earn is influenced by several factors, including the total amount staked within the network and the specific protocol's reward structure. Cryptocurrencies like Ethereum 2.0 often offer higher yields initially to incentivize early participation, but these rates can fluctuate as the network matures and more participants join. Cardano and Polkadot adjust their reward rates based on network conditions and user engagement. It emphasizes the importance of staying informed about the updated developments, allowing you to make informed decisions and stay ahead in the staking game.

Staking requirements and accessibility also play a pivotal role in determining which cryptocurrency might be right for you. Some networks require a significant upfront investment, such as Ethereum's 32 ETH for standalone validators, which might be prohibitive for some investors. However, many platforms have democratized access by allowing smaller contributions through staking pools. This collective approach enables more people to participate without needing extensive technical expertise or significant capital. Cardano's and Polkadot's lower entry barriers make them appealing to a broader audience, providing opportunities to earn rewards without the need for deep pockets or advanced tech knowledge.

Beyond individual gains, staking can profoundly impact a cryptocurrency's community and ecosystem. Participating in staking often involves engaging with the network's governance, where your stake gives you a voice in proposals and decisions. This engagement fosters a sense of ownership and responsibility, encouraging a more active and informed community. For example, Cardano's governance model empowers ADA holders to vote on network upgrades and funding initiatives, directly influencing the blockchain's future direction. Additionally, staking supports the growth of decentralized applications and services, as a secure and vibrant ecosystem attracts developers and innovators. This symbiotic relationship between staking and ecosystem development drives the overall health and expansion of the cryptocurrency network, benefiting all participants involved.

6.3 Calculating Returns: Understanding Your Passive Income

Calculating your potential returns is crucial when considering staking as a source of passive income. It's not just about staking your coins and waiting for rewards—understanding how those rewards are determined can help you optimize your strategy. At the heart of this calculation are reward formulas, which consider several variables. These include the total amount of your staked assets, the duration of your staking period, the current reward rate offered by the network, and any fees that might be associated with staking. Knowing these variables lets you estimate the rewards you can expect over time.

Compounding interest can also play a significant role in your staking returns. You can increase your principal amount by reinvesting the interest into your staked assets, thus earning even more rewards over time. This compoundment can significantly boost your returns, especially if you stake over a long period. Think of it like a little snowball rolling downhill, gathering more snow. The longer you allow your rewards to compound, the larger your snowball—and your potential returns—become. This approach requires discipline and a long-term view but can be incredibly rewarding.

Several factors can influence your staking income, making it essential to remain informed and adaptable. One such factor is the network participation rate, which refers to the proportion of total tokens staked in the network. As more participants join and stake their assets, the overall reward pool is divided among a larger group, potentially reducing individual returns. Conversely, a higher participation rate often increases network security, which benefits the ecosystem. Additionally, inflation and token supply can impact the actual value of your staking rewards. If the supply of a token increases significantly, the relative value of each token might decrease, affecting the purchasing power of your returns.

Look at real-world examples to understand how staking returns can play out in practice. Take an investor who decided to stake their Tezos (XTZ) holdings two years ago. By carefully selecting a reliable validator and reinvesting their earned rewards, they managed to double their initial investment. This example highlights the power of patience and strategic reinvestment. On the other hand, some investors need help choosing less reputable validators, leading to reduced returns or even partial loss of staked assets. These lessons underline the importance of thorough research and strategic planning.

Several tools and resources are available for calculating staking earnings. Online calculators, such as those offered by platforms like StakingRewards.com, provide a straightforward way to estimate gainful earnings based on the amount of coins you're staking, the current reward rate, and your desired staking duration. These calculators can give you a quick snapshot of potential returns, helping you make informed decisions about which assets to stake and for how long. For a more personalized approach, creating a spreadsheet model allows you to input specific variables and projections tailored to your unique situation. This method gives you control over the details and can be adjusted as market conditions change.

As you navigate the complexities of staking, it's clear that understanding and accurately calculating returns is key to maximizing your passive income potential. By considering the factors influencing rewards and utilizing the right tools, you can make proper decisions aligning with your financial goals. This knowledge empowers you as an investor and enhances your engagement with the evolving world of cryptocurrency. As you build your staking strategy, remember that each decision can have a ripple effect, contributing to your overall financial landscape. In the next chapter, we'll explore how to strategically incorporate digital assets into a broader investment portfolio, ensuring that your crypto ventures complement your long-term financial plans.

Chapter 7: Bridging Digital Assets

Envision a future where blockchain networks, often likened to isolated islands, can seamlessly connect, unlocking a realm of possibilities. This future is not a distant dream but a rapidly approaching reality, thanks to the innovation known as bridging. In the crypto context, bridging refers to the technology that enables the transfer of assets across different blockchain networks, addressing one of the significant challenges in the blockchain ecosystem: interoperability. Interoperability is crucial because it allows distinct blockchains to communicate and share information, enabling assets to move freely between them. Imagine the potential of sending Solana coins to an Ethereum wallet; this is now within reach, thanks to bridging. It's a universe where previously separate networks can interconnect, paving the way for a more interconnected and efficient blockchain landscape. The future is bright, and the possibilities are endless.

The technical mechanisms behind bridging are fascinating yet intricate. At the core of this process are smart contracts, automated agreements that govern the bridging process without intermediaries. These smart contracts ensure that the transfer of assets is secure and efficient, minimizing the potential for human error. Also, wrapped tokens play a pivotal role in this ecosystem. When an asset from one blockchain is transferred to another, a wrapped token, a derivative representing the original asset, is created on the target blockchain. This wrapped token is essentially a tokenized version of the original asset, maintaining its value while allowing it to be used on a different blockchain. For instance, if you transfer Bitcoin to the Ethereum network, a Wrapped Bitcoin (WBTC) is created on Ethereum, just like Ether. Like those used in Polkadot's ecosystem, relay chains act as intermediaries facilitating communication and data transfer between blockchains, ensuring that transactions are processed accurately and efficiently.

The benefits of asset bridging are substantial, offering users a range of advantages. One of the primary benefits is the expansion of use cases. By enabling cross-chain transactions, bridging allows users to access a broader array of decentralized applications and services that might not be available on a single network. For instance, you could use a decentralized exchange on the Ethereum network to trade Solana coins or participate in a decentralized finance (DeFi) project on the Binance Smart Chain using assets from the Ethereum network. This access fosters innovation and growth within the blockchain ecosystem, encouraging the development of new and exciting projects.

Furthermore, bridging enhances liquidity by enabling assets to circulate across multiple platforms. This liquidity growth can lead to more efficient markets where assets are traded more efficiently and at reduced costs. As assets flow freely between blockchains, users gain the ability to optimize their holdings, taking advantage of the best opportunities available across different networks.

However, it's crucial to acknowledge that bridging comes with challenges and risks. Security concerns are a significant issue, as the bridging process can introduce vulnerabilities that hackers may exploit. For instance, the Wormhole bridge exploit in early 2022 resulted in substantial losses, highlighting the need for robust security measures. These incidents underscore the importance of thorough audits and consistent monitoring to ensure the safety of cross-chain transactions. Additionally, transaction delays can occur due to the complex nature of cross-chain transfers. These delays may result in latency issues, impacting the speed and efficiency of transactions.

It's essential to remain vigilant and informed, understanding that while bridging offers great potential, it also needs careful consideration of the associated risks. Knowing these risks, you can navigate the blockchain world responsibly and cautiously.

Reflection Section: Bridging Essentials

- Understand the role of smart contracts and wrapped tokens in bridging.

- Recognize the benefits of increased liquidity and expanded use cases.

- Be cautious of the security risks and potential transaction delays.

As you delve into the bridging concept, consider how it can enhance your interaction with the blockchain world. By understanding the mechanisms and benefits, you can make informed decisions about utilizing this technology to optimize your digital assets. Bridging represents a significant step towards a more interconnected and efficient blockchain landscape, and you are at the forefront of this transformation. Understanding and utilizing bridging technology can open new doors for innovation and collaboration, empowering you to navigate the blockchain world confidently. You are not just a fan but an active participant in this exciting journey.

7.2 Popular Bridging Platforms: Pros and Cons

Several platforms stand out when discussing digital asset bridging due to their innovative solutions and widespread adoption. Binance Bridge is a prominent player known for facilitating transfers between Binance Chain and many other blockchains. This bridge supports many cryptocurrencies, making it a versatile tool for users looking to move assets across different networks. Binance Bridge's user-friendly interface caters to beginners and seasoned traders, offering an accessible entry point into cross-chain transactions. The platform boasts robust security measures, with advanced protocols to protect against potential exploits and unauthorized access, ensuring that users can confidently transfer assets.

Polkadot is another leading platform, offering a scalable multi-chain environment that prioritizes interoperability. Through its unique architecture, Polkadot enables different blockchains, or parachains, to interact seamlessly, promoting a cohesive ecosystem. This setup allows Polkadot to support a diverse array of assets and tokens, enhancing its utility for various applications. One of Polkadot's strengths is its speed and efficiency, often processing transactions faster than other networks. However, the complexity of its architecture can pose challenges for users unfamiliar with its intricacies. Moreover, while Polkadot aims to be decentralized, some critics argue that its governance model introduces elements of centralization.

The Cosmos Network takes a different approach by using the Inter-Blockchain Communication (IBC) protocol to connect multiple blockchains. This protocol enables secure and reliable data and asset transfers, fostering a more interconnected blockchain universe. Cosmos supports a broad spectrum of cryptocurrencies, which appeals to those seeking flexibility in their cross-chain activities. Its design emphasizes user experience, providing a straightforward interface simplifying the bridging process. Cosmos faces compatibility challenges despite these advantages, as not all blockchains are IBC-enabled. Additionally, while Cosmos strives for decentralization, the reliance on specific hubs can lead to concerns about potential vulnerabilities or central points of failure.

Each of these platforms has its own set of pros and cons. Binance Bridge, for instance, excels in security and ease of use but may need help with centralization issues due to its custodial nature. Polkadot offers impressive scalability and speed, yet its complex governance and architecture may deter some users. Cosmos brings seamless communication across blockchains but encounters compatibility limitations with networks outside its ecosystem. These factors highlight the importance of understanding users' specific needs and preferences when choosing a bridging platform. Whether prioritizing security, speed, or compatibility, users must weigh these considerations against their goals and risk tolerance.

Security remains an immense concern across all platforms. Each has implemented measures to mitigate risks, such as Binance Bridge's advanced security protocols and Polkadot's shared security model. However, the potential for exploits and vulnerabilities persists, underscoring the need for ongoing vigilance. Transaction speed and cost-effectiveness are also critical factors. Platforms like Polkadot and Cosmos offer efficient processing times, but fees can vary, influencing the overall cost of bridging activities. Users must balance speed and cost benefits against potential security risks and compatibility issues, ensuring their chosen platform aligns with their strategic objectives.

Understanding these platforms' strengths and limitations allows you to make informed decisions regarding digital asset management. You may choose the platform that best meets your criteria by considering factors such as supported assets, user experience, security measures, and potential downsides. Whether you prioritize ease of use, speed, or security, each option offers unique features that can enhance your involvement in the digital asset ecosystem. Exploring these platforms provides valuable insights into blockchain interoperability's dynamic and evolving world.

7.3 Case Studies in Successful Asset Bridging

Successful asset-bridging initiatives highlight the transformative potential of interoperability in the digital asset world. Consider the Ethereum to Binance Smart Chain bridge, a project that has set a precedent for seamless asset movement between two robust blockchain networks. This bridge has been particularly impactful for decentralized finance (DeFi) applications, where users can transfer their Ethereum-based assets to Binance Smart Chain to benefit from lower transaction fees and expedient processing times. This cross-chain transfer is facilitated by creating wrapped tokens that mirror the value of the original Ethereum assets, allowing users to participate in Binance's expanding DeFi ecosystem. The result is a more efficient use of resources and the ability to tap into diverse financial services without being confined to a single blockchain.

Another compelling example comes from the Polkadot ecosystem, where parachains leverage the network's unique interoperability features. Parachains are specialized blockchains that connect to Polkadot's Relay Chain, enabling them to communicate and exchange information seamlessly. A notable project within this framework is Acala. This DeFi-focused parachain has utilized Polkadot's architecture, offering several financial services, including lending, borrowing, and stablecoin issuance. By harnessing Polkadot's shared security model, Acala has ensured high levels of security and performance, providing users with a reliable platform for DeFi activities. This use of parachains demonstrates how Polkadot's design facilitates innovative applications that limit the constraints of traditional blockchain networks.

From these examples, several lessons emerge that are invaluable for those interested in asset bridging:

1. Consider robust security measures. Both projects have implemented stringent security protocols to safeguard against vulnerabilities and protect the integrity of transactions.

2. User-centric design is crucial. These initiatives have focused on creating intuitive interfaces that simplify the bridging process and make it accessible to a broader audience.

3. Overcoming technical and operational challenges has required innovative solutions, such as using relay chains for efficient communication and integrating wrapped tokens to preserve asset value across networks.

These strategies highlight the need for continuous adaptation and improvement in the rapidly evolving blockchain landscape.

The impact of successful asset bridging extends beyond individual users to the broader blockchain ecosystem. For users, the enhanced utility and accessibility of assets mean greater freedom to explore and engage with various applications and services. This increased flexibility encourages active participation in blockchain networks, fostering a vibrant community of developers and users. On a larger scale, successful bridging initiatives contribute to ecosystem growth by facilitating the flow of assets and information across networks. This interconnectedness leads to the development of new projects and applications that leverage the strengths of multiple blockchains, driving innovation and expanding the possibilities of what blockchain technology can achieve.

Several trends and innovations are shaping the asset-bridging landscape. Cross-chain protocols are at the forefront, promising improved interoperability and seamless asset transfers. These protocols aim to standardize communication between blockchains, reducing the complexity and risk associated with bridging. Additionally, the rise of decentralized bridges represents a shift away from centralized control, offering users greater autonomy and security. These innovations pave the way for a more decentralized and interconnected blockchain ecosystem, where assets can move freely and securely across networks. While technologies continue to evolve, they can redefine the boundaries of digital finance and release new opportunities for users and developers alike.

As we conclude this chapter, the exploration of asset bridging reveals its pivotal role in advancing blockchain technology. By studying successful case studies and emerging trends, we see how bridging is not just about connecting blockchains but also about fostering innovation and growth. As we move forward, these insights will guide our understanding of how investors can leverage digital assets to their fullest potential. In the next chapter, we will delve into the strategic use of digital assets in investment portfolios, exploring how they can complement traditional financial strategies and contribute to long-term financial goals.

Chapter 8: Retirement Planning with Crypto

Imagine an artist who seamlessly blends traditional techniques with modern digital tools to create a masterpiece. Similarly, integrating cryptocurrency into your retirement portfolio can offer a unique fusion of traditional and innovative investment strategies. This approach diversifies your portfolio and positions you to take advantage of the dynamic opportunities that digital currencies present. Including cryptocurrencies in your retirement plan can be a game-changer, offering diversification benefits and acting as a hedge against inflation. By adding non-correlated assets like crypto, you can reduce overall portfolio risk. This diversification is crucial, especially in today's volatile markets where traditional assets alone may not suffice. Cryptocurrencies also serve as a potential safeguard against currency devaluation. As more fiat currencies face inflation, digital currencies like Bitcoin and Ethereum offer a store of value that remains unaffected by central bank policies.

A strategic investment framework is essential to integrate crypto into your retirement planning. Start by considering asset allocation models that balance cryptocurrencies with traditional investments such as stocks and bonds. This balance ensures that your portfolio remains robust and can withstand market fluctuations across different asset classes. Allocating a modest percentage of your portfolio, typically between 1% and 5%, to cryptocurrencies can enhance diversification without exposing you to excessive risk. Younger investors with a longer time horizon might consider a slightly higher allocation, potentially up to 10%, as suggested by financial advisors (Source 1). It's essential to evaluate the risk profile of various cryptocurrencies carefully. Not all digital assets are similar, and understanding their volatility, market trends, and underlying technology is crucial. By evaluating these factors, you can make informed decisions that align with your financial goals.

When selecting applicable cryptocurrencies for your retirement portfolio, focus on those that align with long-term investment objectives. Blue-chip cryptocurrencies like Bitcoin and Ethereum are excellent because of their established track record and widespread adoption. With its limited supply and robust security, Bitcoin has become a digital gold standard, while Ethereum's innovative contract capabilities and DeFi applications continue to drive innovation and growth. But don't overlook the potential of emerging projects with strong fundamentals. Cryptocurrencies like Solana and Cardano are gaining traction with their scalable technology and developer-friendly ecosystems (Source 2). These projects promise potential returns and a sense of excitement and adventure for those willing to explore beyond the established titans. They contribute to a diversified crypto portfolio by offering exposure to different blockchain technologies and use cases.

Navigating the tax implications and regulatory environment of crypto retirement investments requires diligence. Tax-advantaged accounts like IRAs or 401(k)s can provide significant benefits. Bitcoin IRAs, for instance, offer tax deductions on contributions, with taxes applied upon withdrawal at retirement for traditional accounts (Source 3). On the other hand, Roth IRAs allow for tax-free withdrawals at retirement, making them attractive for those expecting to be in a higher tax bracket. Understanding these accounts' specific tax treatments and limitations is essential for optimizing your retirement strategy.

Additionally, staying informed about evolving regulations is critical. The regulatory landscape for cryptocurrency is constantly changing, and being proactive about compliance requirements can prevent potential pitfalls. Engaging with financial advisors knowledgeable about crypto investments will ensure that your retirement strategy remains compliant and effective.

Incorporating cryptocurrency into retirement planning is akin to weaving a new thread into an existing tapestry. It necessitates careful consideration and a willingness to embrace innovation while respecting traditional investment principles. Mixing your portfolio with digital assets, you hedge against potential risks and open the door to new growth opportunities. But remember, the key to a successful retirement strategy lies in diversification, balance, informed decision-making, and adaptability in the face of an ever-evolving financial landscape. This strategic approach can enhance your financial security, enhancing a robust foundation for your retirement years. As you explore the possibilities of crypto in your retirement plan, rest assured that you're not just investing but crafting a resilient and adaptable strategy for your future.

Interactive Element: Crypto Retirement Planning Checklist

- Assess your risk tolerance and determine the proper diversification of your portfolio to allocate to cryptocurrencies.

- Research and select established and emerging cryptocurrencies that align with your long-term investment goals.

- Explore tax-advantaged accounts like Bitcoin IRAs and understand their benefits and limitations.

- Stay updated about the latest regulatory developments and compliance requirements in the crypto space.

- Consult a financial advisor experienced in cryptocurrency investments to tailor your retirement strategy.

8.2 Allocating Extra Funds: Investing What You Can Afford to Lose

Imagine your financial life as a sturdy ship navigating unpredictable seas. Risk management serves as the compass in this scenario, guiding you through uncertain waters. The principle of only investing disposable income in high-risk assets like cryptocurrency is not just advice—it's a lifeline. Prioritizing securing your financial safety net first means ensuring your essential expenses and emergency funds are intact before venturing into volatile investments. This strategy protects you from financial distress, allowing you to invest in crypto without jeopardizing your basic needs. Understanding your risk tolerance is equally essential. Ask yourself how much loss you can handle without losing sleep. This self-awareness helps define the boundaries of your investment decisions, ensuring they align with your comfort levels.

Determining how much extra capital to allocate to cryptocurrencies involves a thoughtful approach. A standard guideline is allocating a small percentage of your investment portfolio to high-risk assets. For many, this might mean starting with about 1% to 5%, gradually increasing as you gain confidence and experience. This percentage is a buffer, preventing you from overexposing your finances to the crypto market's inherent volatility. Consider adopting a gradual investment approach, entering the market in phases rather than all at once. This phased entry helps mitigate the impact of market fluctuations, allowing you to adjust your strategy based on real-time conditions. By spreading your investments over time, you can average the purchase price and reduce the risk of buying at a peak.

Investing isn't just a financial endeavor; it's a psychological one. The emotional and psychological factors involved in high-volatility assets like crypto can be overwhelming. Building emotional resilience is crucial when navigating market fluctuations. Prepare yourself for the ups and downs, understanding that volatility is part of the journey. Develop decision-making discipline to avoid impulsive actions driven by market sentiment. Emotional reactions can lead to rash decisions, often resulting in buying high and selling low. Otherwise, focus on your long-term goals and stick to your investment plan, regardless of short-term market noise. By maintaining a cool head, you can make proper decisions that align with your financial objectives.

Regularly reviewing and adjusting your crypto investment strategy is a must. The market doesn't stand still, and neither should your approach. Performance evaluation is key to understanding how your investments are doing. Analyze your returns periodically, assessing whether your allocations need tweaking. This analysis helps you identify what's working and what isn't, enabling you to refine your strategy for better outcomes. Monitor market conditions, adapting to evolving trends and economic factors. Flexibility in your choices allows you to capitalize on new opportunities while minimizing potential risks. Remember, the crypto landscape is dynamic, and staying updated is your best accessory for navigating it successfully.

8.3 Long-term Growth: Balancing Stability and Potential

When thinking about long-term growth in cryptocurrency, a steady, patient approach can often be your best ally. One effective strategy is simply holding onto your assets, a practice widely known as HODLing. You ride out the market's short-term volatility by having your assets for an extended period. This strategy is particularly beneficial in the crypto world, where price swings can be dramatic and frequent. By steadfastly keeping your assets, you give them time to increase value, potentially driven by adoption and technological advancements. Many investors who adopted this approach with Bitcoin and Ethereum have seen significant returns over the years as these assets gained widespread acceptance and utility.

Reinvesting your returns is another powerful tool for long-term growth, which involves taking the profits you earn from your crypto investments and putting them back into the market. It's the financial equivalent of planting seeds to grow a larger crop. By compounding your gains, you increase your potential for future profits. This strategy requires discipline, as it might be tempting to cash out your earnings, especially during bull markets. However, consistently reinvesting enhances your portfolio's growth potential, making it more resilient over time. This compounding effect can be particularly impactful in the crypto market, where even small, continuous investments can lead to substantial growth.

Stablecoins provide a stable foundation within your crypto retirement portfolio, balancing risk and security. These digital assets are pegged to traditional currencies, such as the US dollar, which helps mitigate overall portfolio volatility. You create a buffer that protects your portfolio from the market's wild fluctuations by including stablecoins. They also offer opportunities for yield generation through lending platforms. By lending your stablecoins, you can earn interest, adding another layer of income to your retirement plan. This dual role makes stablecoins an attractive option for those looking to balance growth with stability, allowing you to maintain liquidity and flexibility.

Technological advancements play a critical role in shaping the long-term potential of crypto investments. Blockchain upgrades, for instance, can significantly impact asset values. As networks improve, with faster transaction speeds and enhanced security features, the value of the underlying assets often increases. These upgrades not only improve user experience but also drive broader adoption, which in turn boosts demand and price. Adoption trends are equally important. As cryptocurrencies become more integrated into everyday life, their mainstream acceptance grows. This acceptance can spur further innovation and investment, delivering a positive feedback loop that benefits long-term investors.

Continuous monitoring and adaptation ensure your portfolio remains aligned with market developments. Financial indicators like inflation and interest rates can affect crypto prices. By analyzing these factors, you can anticipate potential market shifts and adjust your strategy accordingly. Staying informed about regulatory shifts is also crucial. Changes in crypto regulations can impact market dynamics, influencing liquidity and valuations. By being proactive and adaptable, you can navigate these changes effectively, ensuring your portfolio remains resilient in the face of evolving market conditions. This vigilance allows you to seize new opportunities while safeguarding your investments against unforeseen challenges.

Thus, a thoughtful approach to long-term crypto growth involves a combination of strategic holding, reinvestment, and diversification through stablecoins. You can capitalize on technological advancements and market changes by staying informed and adaptable, building a robust and forward-thinking retirement portfolio. As you integrate these strategies, remember that balance is key—balancing risk with reward and stability with potential. The next chapter will explore how to navigate common crypto challenges, equipping you with the tools and knowledge needed to thrive in the complex world of digital assets.

Chapter 9: Overcoming Common Crypto Challenges

Picture yourself standing at the edge of a vast, unpredictable ocean, its waves crashing with fury and calm; it's the cryptocurrency market—a place of immense opportunity and equal uncertainty. As you navigate these digital waters, the ever-present volatility challenge looms large. Cryptocurrency markets are notorious for their turbulent price swings, which are far more pronounced than traditional financial markets. These swings, however, also signify the potential for significant growth and innovation, attributed to several factors, including market sentiment, liquidity levels, and the nascent nature of the crypto space. Understanding volatility is essential for anyone hoping to thrive in this environment.

At the heart of crypto volatility lies market sentiment. News, events, and the emotions of investors can significantly sway prices. A single tweet from a prominent figure or a new regulation can trigger dramatic market reactions, compounded by the presence of less informed retail investors, whose decisions often reflect broader emotional trends rather than rational analysis. As a result, crypto markets can experience rapid, unpredictable movements. Liquidity levels also play a critical role in amplifying price swings. The crypto market, though growing, remains relatively small compared to traditional financial markets. This limited liquidity means large trades can significantly impact prices, leading to greater volatility.

Developing emotional resilience is a crucial skill for navigating the cryptocurrency market. It's easy to be swept away by the market's highs and lows, but maintaining composure is key to making sound investment decisions. Mindfulness techniques, such as meditation, can help reduce stress and keep you grounded. Setting emotional boundaries is equally important. Avoid overexposure to market news and constant price checks, which can lead to anxiety and impulsive decisions. By stepping back and maintaining a balanced perspective, you can approach the market with clarity and confidence.

Implementing volatility mitigation strategies can further protect your investments. Stop-loss orders are valuable, allowing you to set predefined exit points to limit potential losses. You can prevent emotional decision-making during market downturns by automatically selling an asset if it falls to a specific price. Hedging is another strategy that can offset potential losses in volatile markets. It involves using derivatives, like future and option contracts, to protect against adverse price movements. These strategies require careful planning and understanding but add a safety net in an unpredictable market.

Focusing on long-term goals can provide a sense of direction and stability in the stormy seas of cryptocurrency volatility. Shifting your perspective from short-term price movements to long-term investment objectives is essential. Historical market cycles provide valuable context, showing how markets have recovered and grown over time. This historical perspective can reassure you during periods of volatility, reminding you that market fluctuations are often temporary. Aligning your investment strategies with your financial endeavors and time horizon is equally essential. Concentrating on the larger picture allows you to navigate the market with patience and purpose, making decisions that support your long-term aspirations.

Reflection Section: Navigating Volatility

Take a moment to reflect on your emotional responses to market fluctuations. How do you typically react to news of a market crash or a sudden price surge? Consider practicing mindfulness techniques to cultivate emotional resilience. Review your investment strategy to ensure it includes volatility mitigation measures such as stop-loss orders or hedging. Please write down your thoughts and strategies for handling volatility and refer back to them during market turbulence.

As you continue to explore the cryptocurrency world, remember that volatility is both a challenge and an opportunity. By understanding its nature and implementing strategies to manage it, you can navigate the market with greater confidence and resilience.

9.2 Simplifying Crypto Jargon: Breaking Down the Language Barrier

Navigating the world of cryptocurrency can feel like learning a new language. Terms like "blockchain" and "altcoins" pop up frequently; knowing these terms can significantly affect how you perceive and engage with digital assets. At its core, a blockchain is a decentralized digital ledger. Imagine a digital notebook that records transactions across numerous computers simultaneously. This setup ensures that it's nearly impossible to alter once data is recorded without the network's consensus, providing security and transparency. Altcoins represent the multitude of cryptocurrencies beyond Bitcoin. They range from Ethereum to lesser-known coins, each offering unique features and uses. HODL, originating from a misspelled word in a forum post, now stands for "Hold On for Dear Life." It reflects a strategy of holding onto cryptocurrencies long-term, regardless of short-term price fluctuations, embodying a belief in the asset's future potential.

Breaking down technical concepts into layperson's terms is crucial for demystifying crypto. Smart contracts are essentially self-executing agreements. They routinely enforce and execute the terms of a contract written into code, eliminating the need for intermediaries. Think of them as digital agreements that execute themselves when certain conditions are specific, ensuring trust and efficiency. Mining involves validating transactions and aggregating new blocks onto the blockchain. Miners use high-tech computers to solve complex mathematical problems, secure the network, and earn cryptocurrency as a reward. Gas fees are the costs associated with transactions on a blockchain. Just like paying for fuel to drive a car, users pay these fees to power operations on the network, ensuring transactions are processed smoothly and efficiently.

To help bridge the knowledge gap, creating a crypto glossary can be invaluable. Such a glossary would offer an alphabetical listing of terms and definitions, providing a quick reference guide for anyone navigating this complex field. For instance, under "B," you might find "blockchain," accompanied by a brief definition and a practical example of how it functions in everyday crypto transactions. Contextual examples are essential for illustrating term usage, providing clarity, and enhancing understanding. Imagine reading about "gas fees" and seeing an example of how they affect the total cost of transferring Ethereum. These real-world applications ground the terminology, making it easier to grasp the fundamental concepts that drive the crypto ecosystem.

Ongoing education is not just a decision but a necessity in the fast-paced world of digital currencies. The landscape evolves quickly, with new terms and technologies emerging regularly. Engaging with the crypto community is a fantastic way to stay informed and expand your understanding. Online platforms like Coursera and Udemy offer structured courses that delve into various aspects of cryptocurrency, from blockchain basics to advanced trading strategies. These platforms can provide a solid foundation and update you on the latest developments. Community forums, such as Reddit and Bitcointalk, are vibrant spaces where enthusiasts and experts alike share insights, discuss trends, and provide answers to questions. Participating in these discussions enhances your knowledge and keeps you engaged and motivated in the ever-evolving crypto space.

As you immerse yourself in this world, remember that learning is a continuous process. The more you engage, the more you'll understand the intricacies of cryptocurrency.

9.3 Avoiding Scams: Due Diligence and Red Flags

In the digital realm of cryptocurrency, the promise of high returns can often blind even the most cautious among us. But beneath the glittering facade lies a minefield of scams that prey on both the inexperienced and the seasoned investor. One of the most notorious scams in the crypto space is the Ponzi scheme. These schemes entice investors with promises of high returns with little risk. They rely on recruiting new participants to pay returns to earlier investors, creating a cycle that collapses when recruitment slows. The allure of quick wealth can be tempting, but understanding the mechanics of a Ponzi scheme can help you steer clear.

Phishing attacks represent another significant threat. These attacks involve cybercriminals masquerading as trustworthy entities to steal sensitive information. They might send messages and emails that could be legitimate but aim to trick you into revealing passwords or private keys. Always verify the source of any request for personal information and be wary of clicking on links or downloading attachments from unknown senders. Fake Initial Coin Offerings (ICOs) are yet another pitfall. Fraudsters create these bogus ICOs to promote funds for schemes, leaving investors with worthless tokens. Before investing, scrutinize the project's legitimacy and demand transparency.

Pump and dump schemes are particularly insidious in the crypto world. Here, unscrupulous actors artificially inflate the price of a cryptocurrency through misleading statements. When the price is sufficiently high, they sell off their holdings, causing the price to plummet and leaving late investors with significant losses. Staying informed and skeptical can protect you from falling prey to such tactics. Conducting thorough due diligence is your first line of defense against these scams. Start by analyzing a project's whitepaper—the document that outlines the project's goals, technology, and plans. A well-written, detailed whitepaper is a good sign, but not a guarantee. Look for clarity and specificity in the project's objectives.

Team verification is equally vital. Investigate the backgrounds and credibility of the project founders and development team. Check their previous work, professional history, and reputation within the crypto community. Community feedback is another crucial component. Engage with online forums and discussions to gauge public opinion and gather insights from other investors. Platforms like Reddit and Bitcointalk can be invaluable resources for gathering diverse perspectives. Recognizing red flags can save you from potential financial disaster. Be cautious of projects that promise unrealistic returns. While high returns are possible in crypto, guarantees are a significant warning sign.

Transparency is another critical factor. Legitimate projects should provide clear and comprehensive information about their operations, goals, and financials. If a project is vague or evasive, consider it a red flag. Poor communication from project representatives also signals trouble. If responses to inquiries are limited or evasive, this may indicate a lack of professionalism or integrity. Implementing risk mitigation strategies can further shield you from scams. Diversifying your portfolio lessens the impact of any single investment loss. By spreading investments across various assets, you minimize risk and increase the potential for gains.

Use reputable exchanges to conduct transactions. Platforms like Coinbase and Binance offer robust security measures and have established reputations, reducing the likelihood of encountering fraudulent activity. Enabling security features like two-factor authentication (2FA) protects your accounts, making unauthorized access more difficult. As you navigate the crypto landscape, remember that vigilance and skepticism are your best allies. By understanding common scams, conducting due diligence, recognizing red flags, and implementing risk mitigation strategies, you can protect your investments and make informed decisions.

In the bigger picture, safeguarding your assets protects your financial future and contributes to a more secure and trustworthy crypto ecosystem. As we move forward, the next chapter will delve into the practical tools and platforms that enhance your trading experience, providing you with the means to refine your strategies further and execute them effectively.

Chapter 10: Future Trends in Cryptocurrency

Envision a world where the lines between physical and digital realities dissolve, ushering in a realm brimming with fresh opportunities and experiences. This is the metaverse, an expansive digital universe where virtual environments thrive, and users engage in ways that were once confined to the realm of science fiction. Giants like Meta, formerly known as Facebook, have poured billions into shaping this digital landscape, underscoring its capability to revolutionize our interaction with technology. The metaverse is not just a passing fad—it's a profound shift in our perception and participation in digital spaces, offering a plethora of avenues for exploration and investment.

The metaverse is a complex and multifaceted environment comprising virtual worlds where users can interact in immersive digital settings. These worlds are crafted with meticulous attention to detail, providing spaces where individuals can socialize, work, and play. Augmented Reality (AR) integration further enhances these experiences by integrating digital elements into the real world, creating a hybrid reality that enriches everyday interactions. Imagine attending a meeting where holographic presentations hover before you or playing a game where your living room becomes the battlefield. This blending of realities opens new avenues for creativity and connection, making the metaverse a compelling space for personal and professional engagement.

Investment opportunities within the metaverse are as diverse as the environments it encompasses. Virtual real estate has become lucrative, with digital lands and properties bought and sold for substantial sums. Platforms like Decentraland and The Sandbox lead this charge, offering users the chance to own parcels of digital land where they can build, host events, or even lease spaces to others. These virtual properties are not just static assets; they generate income and appreciation, much like physical real estate. Additionally, the trade of digital goods and services is thriving within these virtual ecosystems. Users can buy and sell virtual clothing, art, and experiences, creating an economy that mirrors the real world but operates entirely in the digital domain.

The innovation potential truly shines at the intersection of cryptocurrencies and the metaverse. Cryptocurrencies and blockchain technology are the backbone of metaverse economies, facilitating secure and transparent transactions. Tokenization, a key concept, allows users to represent ownership of digital assets and properties through tokens. To put it simply, tokens are like digital certificates that prove you own something in the metaverse. These tokens can be bought and sold on decentralized marketplaces, enabling peer-to-peer transactions without intermediaries. This decentralization is crucial, as it empowers users to have complete control over their digital assets, fostering an environment of trust and autonomy. In the metaverse, blockchain ensures that ownership is verifiable and immutable, providing a foundation for a thriving digital economy.

The cultural and societal impacts of the metaverse are profound, reshaping how we define identity and community in the digital age. In virtual worlds, users can craft digital personas and avatars, expressing themselves in ways that transcend physical limitations. This ability to shape one's identity fosters a new level of creativity and self-exploration, allowing individuals to experience different facets of themselves. Additionally, the metaverse catalyzes community building, offering platforms where people from diverse backgrounds can connect and collaborate. These digital communities are not bound by geography, enabling the formation of global networks that challenge traditional notions of social interaction.

Reflection Section: Metaverse and You

Consider how the metaverse could influence your personal and professional life. For instance, in your personal life, you could use the metaverse to socialize with friends and family who are far away, or to attend virtual events and concerts. In your professional life, you could use the metaverse for virtual meetings and conferences, or to collaborate with colleagues in a virtual workspace. Manifest the potential benefits and challenges of engaging with virtual realities. How might you leverage these opportunities for growth and connection? Write down your thoughts and explore how the metaverse could affect your future endeavors.

10.2 Web3 Innovations: What's Next for the Internet?

Web3 is not a mere buzzword; it represents a significant leap in our internet interaction. At the core of Web3 are innovations like decentralized identity and self-sovereign data. These concepts are reshaping how we manage our digital presence. A decentralized identity empowers you to control your digital persona, eliminating the need for multiple passwords and reducing the risk of data breaches. Imagine having a single digital identity you own, which grants you access to services without compromising personal data to third parties. This shift puts you in the driver's seat, wresting control from centralized entities that often misuse personal information for profit.

Self-sovereign data takes this empowerment further by allowing you to own and manage your personal information independently. Privacy is continually compromised; therefore, this innovation is crucial. It means you decide what data you share and with whom. No longer will your data be a commodity traded without your consent. Instead, it becomes a personal asset that you control. This change is monumental, especially in an age where data is as valuable as currency. By giving you the tools to manage your data, Web3 fosters a more equitable digital landscape where individuals can engage without fear of exploitation.

The impact of Web3 on internet infrastructure is profound. Distributed ledger technology, a blockchain cornerstone, enhances online transactions' security and transparency. This technology ensures that every transaction on a public ledger is recorded and visible to all but alterable by none. This transparency builds trust, as you can verify transactions independently. It also enhances security by making fraud and manipulation nearly impossible.

Additionally, mesh networks are decentralizing internet connectivity, improving resilience and reliability. These networks distribute data across multiple nodes, ensuring that others continue to function if one fails. This redundancy protects against outages and censorship, creating a more open and accessible internet for everyone.

Privacy and security have always been concerns on the internet, but Web3 addresses these with advanced solutions. Zero-knowledge proofs offer privacy-preserving verification methods, allowing you to prove information without revealing it. For instance, you could verify your age without disclosing your birthdate. This technology maintains your privacy while ensuring security. Enhanced encryption further protects your data, using sophisticated cryptographic techniques to prevent unauthorized access. These advancements safeguard your information, ensuring that your online interactions remain private and secure, even in a digital age where cyber threats are prevalent.

Web3's influence extends to digital economies, reshaping business models and financial interactions. Decentralized Finance (DeFi) is expanding, broadening access to financial services by removing traditional barriers. With DeFi, you can borrow and earn interest without a bank. This democratization of finance opens opportunities to a broader audience, fostering financial inclusion. Additionally, token-based economies are emerging, incentivizing participation through digital rewards. Tokens can portray anything from ownership in a company to a stake in a community project. This system encourages engagement and collaboration, creating vibrant digital ecosystems where everyone has a role. These changes are redefining economic interactions, paving the way for more inclusive and dynamic digital marketplaces.

10.3 Predicting Future Market Shifts: Staying Ahead of the Curve

Understanding the ebb and flow of cryptocurrency markets requires more than intuition; it demands a keen eye for historical patterns. By examining past market behaviors, we can identify the cyclical nature of up and down markets. These cycles are not random; they follow specific trends and indicators. During a bull market, optimism drives prices up, often fueled by technological advancements or increased adoption. Investors flock to buy, expecting continued growth.

Conversely, bear markets bring a more somber mood, often triggered by regulatory concerns or economic downturns. Prices fall as investors sell off assets, seeking to minimize losses. Recognizing these cycles helps you anticipate shifts and position yourself strategically. The adoption curve further informs us by highlighting the stages of technology acceptance, from early adopters to mainstream users. Each phase has dynamics, influencing market behavior and providing clues about future directions.

Data analytics and artificial intelligence (AI) have become apparent as powerful tools for forecasting market trends in the digital age. Machine learning models, for instance, analyze vast datasets to identify patterns and predictive signals that human eyes might miss. These algorithms continually learn from new data, refining their predictions over time. They can forecast price movements by recognizing correlations that are not immediately apparent. Meanwhile, sentiment analysis gauges market mood by sifting through social media posts, news articles, and other online content. By assessing the tone and context of these communications, AI can provide insights into investor sentiment, helping predict market trends. This combination of data-driven intelligence offers a more nuanced understanding of market dynamics, enhancing your ability to make informed investment decisions.

Emerging technologies are poised to reshape the crypto market landscape, with quantum computing and interoperability protocols leading the charge. Quantum computing promises unprecedented computational power, which could revolutionize blockchain security and efficiency. This technology could crack current encryption methods, prompting the development of quantum-resistant algorithms to protect digital assets. On the other hand, interoperability protocols are breaking down barriers between different blockchain networks. These protocols enable seamless cross-chain interactions, facilitating collaboration and resource sharing. This interconnectedness promises to enhance the versatility and functionality of blockchain applications, driving innovation across industries. Keeping afloat of these technological advancements is crucial for staying competitive in the ever-evolving crypto market.

In an unpredictable market, adaptability is key to success. Developing investment strategies that can pivot in response to changing conditions is vital. Scenario planning, for example, involves preparing for a range of market outcomes, from bullish trends to potential downturns. By considering various scenarios, you can devise plans that protect your investments while capitalizing on opportunities. Diversification is another critical tactic. Spreading your investments across different asset classes reduces risk and increases potential returns. By not relying on a single asset or market, you can weather fluctuations more effectively, ensuring a more stable portfolio. These adaptive strategies empower you to maneuver the complexities of the crypto market with assurance and resilience.

As we wrap up this chapter, remember that predicting market shifts involves a blend of historical insight, technological awareness, and strategic planning. By staying informed and flexible, you can position yourself to thrive in the dynamic world of cryptocurrency. In the next chapter, we will delve into engaging with real-world applications, exploring how these technologies are already transforming industries and offering new opportunities for growth and innovation.

Chapter 11: Engaging with Real-world Applications

Imagine a crowded stock exchange floor, but instead of paper and frantic shouting, there are digital screens and a quiet hum of algorithms. In digital asset trading, fortunes can change with a single click. Learning from those who have successfully traded can be invaluable as you navigate this space. Let's delve into some case studies of significant crypto trades, examining the strategies that led to impressive returns. The thrill of a successful trade, the rush of making the right decision in a volatile market, is an experience that can't be matched.

Take the Bitcoin bull run of 2017, for instance. It was a time of euphoria, with Bitcoin's price skyrocketing from around $1,000 to almost $20,000 by the end of the year. Traders capitalizing on this surge often employed a mix of technical analysis and market sentiment. They observed breaking resistance levels and confirming bullish trends, using tools like Moving Average Convergence Divergence (MACD) and Relative Strength Index (RSI) to spot entry points. The key was patience and timing—waiting for the right moment as the market built momentum. This strategic approach, coupled with a keen understanding of market conditions, allowed them to make the most of the market's upward trend.

Similarly, Ethereum's Initial Coin Offering (ICO) boom presented a unique opportunity. Investors recognized the potential of Ethereum's platform beyond its role as a cryptocurrency. They saw it as a foundation for decentralized applications and smart contracts. Participating in early ICOs gave them access to tokens that would later see substantial appreciation. These investors understood the importance of assessing a project's fundamentals, such as the team behind it, the problem it aimed to solve, and its market potential. This strategic foresight and due diligence allowed them to reap significant rewards as the ICO market exploded.

Successful crypto traders often employ specific strategies that are worth noting. Scalping is a technique where traders make rapid trades to gain small profits from minor price movements. It necessitates a keen understanding of market trends and technical indicators and the ability to execute trades quickly. Position trading, on the other hand, involves holding onto assets for more extended periods, often based on macroeconomic trends or long-term growth potential. This strategy appeals to those confident in their analysis and willing to weather short-term volatility for more significant long-term gains.

What sets successful traders apart are the traits they cultivate. Effective risk management is crucial. Setting clear stop-loss limits helps control potential losses, ensuring that a single bad trade doesn't wipe out their portfolio. Additionally, successful traders commit to continuous learning. They stay updated about the latest market developments, technological advancements, and regulatory changes, constantly updating their techniques to adapt to the ever-evolving outlook of cryptocurrency trading. This dedication to learning and staying updated is a key factor in their success.

Mistakes are inevitable in trading, but learning from them is what drives success. Overtrading, or making too many trades in a short period, is a common pitfall. It can lead to negative decision-making and increased transaction costs, ultimately eroding profits. Successful traders recognize this danger and maintain discipline, focusing on quality over quantity. Emotional decision-making is another challenge. The crypto market is highly volatile, and it's easy to get swept up in the excitement of rising prices or the fear of sudden drops. Successful traders learn to maintain objectivity, relying on data and analysis rather than emotions to guide their decisions.

Reflection Section: Trading Self-Assessment

Consider the strategies and traits discussed. Reflect on your trading approach. Do you set clear limits to manage risk? How do you ensure your decisions remain objective? Take a moment to jot down your thoughts and identify areas for improvement.

11.2 Real-life Staking Success Stories

Picture yourself participating in a vibrant community where your contribution benefits you and strengthens the network; it's the essence of staking in the cryptocurrency world. Let's explore how real individuals have leveraged staking to achieve notable success, starting with Cardano staking pools. Imagine an operator who saw the potential in Cardano's proof-of-stake model early on. They gathered a group of like-minded individuals to pool their resources by creating a staking pool. This collective effort allowed them to secure the network and earn rewards distributed among participants. Their success wasn't just in the returns but in building a thriving community where everyone had a stake in the network's success. By focusing on transparency and regular communication, they gained trust and attracted more members, amplifying their pool's influence and rewards.

Similarly, Polkadot nominators have made their mark by consistently earning rewards through strategic participation. Here, individuals nominate trustworthy validators to secure the network, effectively lending their stake to those they believe will act honestly and efficiently. By carefully selecting validators based on reputation and performance metrics, nominators enhance their earnings and contribute to the network's security. This process cultivates a sense of responsibility and engagement, as each nominator's decision impacts the network's overall health. The stories of these nominators are filled with tales of due diligence as they navigate the dynamic landscape of validators, always on the lookout for those who align with their values and objectives.

Strategies vary widely in the realm of staking, offering different paths to success. Solo staking involves individuals operating their validator nodes, granting them complete control over their staked assets. While this method provides greater autonomy and potentially higher rewards, it requires significant technical expertise and resources to maintain a reliable node. On the other hand, pool staking allows participants to combine their resources with others, reducing individual risk and technical demands. This communal approach fosters collaboration and shared success as participants benefit from the collective power of the pool.

Reinvestment strategies play a crucial role in maximizing staking returns. Individuals can amplify their earnings over time by compounding their earned rewards into their staked assets. This approach requires discipline and a long-term perspective, as the benefits of compounding become more pronounced with patience. Successful takers often adopt a systematic approach, regularly evaluating their returns and adjusting their reinvestment strategies based on market conditions and personal goals. This proactive mindset lets them adapt and thrive despite market fluctuations.

The impact of community and collaboration within staking cannot be overstated. Engaging in community governance allows stakeholders to participate in decision-making, influencing the direction of the network and ensuring their voices matter. This involvement fosters a sense of ownership and accountability, as stakers take an active role in shaping the future of the network. Knowledge sharing further enhances this collaborative spirit, as stakers exchange insights, advice, and best practices with one another. They build support and friendship networks through forums, social media groups, and dedicated platforms, empowering each other to succeed tremendously. The sense of community and support in staking is a powerful motivator and a key to success.

However, staking has its challenges. Network downtime can pose a significant threat, as validator outages may lead to missed opportunities and reduced rewards. Successful stakers mitigate this risk by implementing robust technical solutions, such as redundant systems and failover mechanisms, to ensure their nodes remain operational. They also stay informed about network upgrades and potential disruptions, allowing them to respond quickly and minimize downtime. Slashing risks, where validators are penalized for malicious behavior or technical failures, present another hurdle; by overcoming this, stakers focus on selecting reliable validators and maintaining strict operational standards to avoid penalties. By prioritizing security and reliability, they safeguard their assets and contribute to the network's resilience.

11.3 Integrating Crypto in Everyday Transactions

Consider a world where you can effortlessly use cryptocurrencies for daily purchases; this isn't a distant dream; it's happening now. Imagine paying for your morning coffee with Bitcoin or Ethereum. Retail payments using cryptocurrencies are becoming increasingly common. Businesses like Overstock and some Shopify stores accept digital currencies, making it possible to use crypto just as you would a credit card. This shift is not only about convenience; it's about embracing a new form of currency that offers unique benefits. Cryptocurrencies allow an alternative to traditional payment methods, enabling you to transact globally without needing currency exchange or hefty fees; this is particularly useful for frequent travelers or those who regularly shop from international vendors. The ability to pay with crypto simplifies these transactions, offering a seamless experience that is both modern and efficient.

Sending money across borders has historically been fraught with challenges—high fees, long processing times, and the complexities of currency conversion. Cryptocurrencies are changing that. With digital currencies, you can send remittances to family members in another country almost instantly and at a fraction of the traditional cost. Platforms like Ripple are explicitly designed for cross-border payments, offering a more cost-effective and faster alternative to conventional banking systems. This capability is a game-changer for those who regularly send money overseas, providing a way to support loved ones without the overhead of traditional methods. The speed of crypto transactions also means that the recipient can access funds almost immediately, which is crucial in times of emergency or need. This efficiency and savings make cryptocurrencies an attractive option for international money transfers, democratizing access to global financial resources.

The advantages of using crypto in everyday transactions are manifold. One significant benefit is the reduction of transaction costs. Traditional banking systems often come with several fees—service charges, currency conversion fees, and more. Cryptocurrencies cut out the middleman, allowing for peer-to-peer transactions that significantly lower these costs. This reduction is advantageous for consumers and businesses, as it increases spending more on goods and services rather than fees.

Also, the speed and efficiency of crypto transactions are noteworthy. Unlike traditional bank transfers, which take days to process, crypto transactions are often completed within minutes. This rapid settlement process is particularly beneficial for businesses that rely on quick payment confirmations to maintain cash flow. By integrating crypto into everyday use, individuals and companies can enjoy a streamlined, cost-effective payment method that aligns with modern expectations for speed and efficiency.

Several platforms and services have emerged to facilitate these everyday transactions. Crypto debit cards, for example, are becoming increasingly popular. These cards authorize you to spend your Bitcoin or other cryptocurrencies like cash. At the point of sale, the crypto is converted into fiat currency, making the process seamless for both the consumer and the merchant. Crypto.com and BitPay are leading the charge in this area, offering cards accepted anywhere traditional debit and credit cards are.

Mobile wallets like Coinbase Wallet and Trust Wallet offer convenient ways to manage and use cryptocurrencies. These apps allow you to securely store, send, and receive crypto, making it easy to integrate digital currencies into your daily life. With these mechanisms, you can enjoy the benefits of crypto without the hassle of managing complex transactions or fluctuating exchange rates.

Despite these advancements, challenges to widespread crypto adoption remain. One of the primary barriers is merchant acceptance. While more businesses are beginning to accept cryptocurrencies, many still hesitate due to volatility and regulatory uncertainty concerns. To overcome this, education and awareness are crucial. Businesses require understanding the potential benefits of accepting crypto—lower transaction fees, access to a broader customer base, and the ability to stay ahead of technological trends. Another challenge is user education. For many, the world of crypto can seem daunting or confusing. Simplifying the onboarding process is essential to encourage more people to integrate crypto into their everyday lives, completing this through user-friendly platforms, clear educational resources, and support from the crypto community to guide new users through the initial steps. Addressing these barriers can make way for a future where cryptocurrencies are as commonplace as cash or card transactions, offering a modern, efficient alternative to traditional payment systems.

This chapter explored how crypto can be incorporated into everyday life, offering efficient and cost-effective solutions for retail and remittance transactions. As we look to the future, the potential for cryptocurrencies to simplify and enhance our financial interactions is immense. Next, we'll delve deeper into the emerging technologies that continue to reshape our understanding of value and ownership.

Chapter 12: Understanding and Leveraging Market Trends

Knowing and Leveraging Market Trends is a crucial skill for any investor. It's like standing at the edge of a vast forest, with paths leading in various directions. Each path prompts its own set of challenges and rewards, much like the financial markets. As an investor, your ability to navigate these paths—marked by bull and bear markets—can define your success. In the world of cryptocurrencies, these market trends amplify and offer both more significant opportunities and risks. Understanding the characteristics and indicators of these market phases is crucial. A bull market, identified by rising prices and investor confidence, feels like a wave of prosperity where growth opportunities abound. On the other hand, a bear market signifies a period of declining prices and prevailing pessimism, requiring strategic thinking to protect and possibly even grow your investments.

Bull markets are exhilarating, but they also demand caution. Prices ascend, optimism flourishes, and the air is thick with opportunity. This phase signifies increased demand, high investor confidence, and a positive economic outlook. As prices rise, media attention swells, often accompanied by celebrity endorsements and pop culture influences. For investors, this is the time to capitalize. One of the most straightforward strategies in a bull market is the buy-and-hold approach. This strategy involves purchasing assets and holding onto them for a long period, even as their value increases. The idea is to ride the upward trend to maximize gains. However, it's essential to remain vigilant and not get swept away by the euphoria. Momentum trading is another tactic where you identify and jump on price surges, profiting from short-term upward movements; it requires keen observation and quick decision-making, as the crypto market's volatility can turn the tide rapidly. Diversifying across growth sectors by investing in high-performing altcoins can also enhance returns. These altcoins often experience significant gains during bull runs, providing a lucrative avenue for diversification.

Conversely, bear markets demand a different set of strategies. Prices fall, demand dwindles, and negative sentiment prevails. In this environment, protecting your investments becomes paramount. One effective trading strategy is short selling. Short selling allows you to profit from a downside in the price of an asset. Here's how it works: you borrow an asset, such as a cryptocurrency, from a broker and sell it at the current market price. Then, you watch for the price to drop, buy back the asset at a lesser price, return it to the broker, and make up the difference. This approach allows you to profit from falling prices but requires a deep understanding of market dynamics and timing. Hedging your portfolio with stablecoins is another way to preserve value during downturns. You can shield your investments from market fluctuations by converting volatile assets into stablecoins and pegged to traditional currencies. This stability provides a haven, allowing you to take cover until the market recovers.

Recognizing the transition signals between bull and bear markets is crucial for timely strategy adjustments. Volume analysis is a fundamental tool in this regard. Changes in trading volume often precede trend shifts, acting as an early warning system for market transitions. A sudden increase in volume can indicate a potential reversal, signaling a change in investor sentiment. Moving average crossovers are another valuable indicator. Once a short-term moving (STM) average crosses above a long-term moving(LTM)average, it suggests a potential upward trend, while the opposite crossover indicates a possible decline. These technical indicators empower you to anticipate market fluctuations, enabling you to adjust your strategies accordingly.

Interactive Element: Volume and Moving Averages Exercise

Incorporate volume analysis and moving averages into your trading routine. Monitor a cryptocurrency of your choice over a month, noting changes in volume and moving average crossovers. Record your observations and any market shifts, reflecting on how these indicators align with accurate market movements. This activity will deepen your understanding of technical analysis and enhance your ability to recognize market transitions.

Understanding these phases and employing appropriate strategies can significantly impact investment outcomes as you navigate the crypto market. By recognizing the characteristics of bull and bear markets, developing tailored strategies, and identifying transition signals, you position yourself to leverage opportunities and mitigate risks.

12.2 Recognizing and Capitalizing on Market Trends

Successfully navigating the ever-changing sea of cryptocurrency requires a keen eye for emerging trends. Spotting these trends early can significantly impact your investment strategy. Technological progress plays a significant role in shaping market interest. Innovations like blockchain scalability and privacy enhancements can ignite enthusiasm, attracting more investors. For instance, when Ethereum announced its shift to Ethereum 2.0, the market buzzed excitedly, leading to increased investment. Staying informed about such advancements keeps you ahead, allowing you to position yourself strategically and take advantage of these market shifts.

Regulatory developments play an important role in shaping market dynamics. Governments around the world are grappling with how to regulate digital currencies. New laws can create a conducive growth environment or introduce hurdles that could stifle innovation. Keeping abreast of these regulations is essential as it helps you anticipate potential impacts on market behavior and adjust your strategies accordingly. This understanding gives you a sense of control and security in your investments.

Macroeconomic indicators are equally important. Global economic conditions influence investor sentiment, such as inflation rates, unemployment, and geopolitical tensions. During economic uncertainty, investors often turn to cryptocurrencies as a hedge against traditional financial systems. For example, during the COVID-19 pandemic, many sought refuge in digital assets, leading to a surge in demand. Eyeing these indicators helps you gauge the broader economic landscape, providing insights into potential market shifts. By knowing these factors, you can better predict how they affect cryptocurrency prices and adjust your investments to capitalize on these trends.

Assessing the strength and longevity of market trends is critical. Trendlines and channels serve as visual tools that help you determine the direction and sustainability of a trend. You can identify patterns and potential breakout points by plotting price movements on a chart. These tools allow you to visualize the market's trajectory, making it easier to decide when to enter or exit a trade. The Relative Strength Index is another valuable indicator. It delegates the speed and change of price movements, providing insights into whether an asset is overbought or oversold. An RSI above 70 suggests an overbought condition, indicating a potential price correction, while a Relative Strength Index (RSI) below 30 indicates an oversold condition, signaling a possible upward reversal. Using these tools in tandem can enhance your ability to assess the strength and duration of market trends.

Developing a trend-based trading strategy involves leveraging these insights to create a structured plan. Breakout trading is a popular approach, where you enter positions when prices break key levels, signaling the start of a new trend. This strategy requires patience and vigilance; you must wait for breakout confirmation before committing. Pullback opportunities present another avenue for profit. Here, you buy during temporary price corrections within a broader trend, capitalizing on the market's natural ebb and flow. This approach allows you to enter at a lower price, increasing your potential for returns; combining these strategies, you can create a comprehensive trading plan that adapts to market conditions and maximizes your chances of success.

Utilizing the right tools is essential to recognize and capitalize on market trends effectively. Technical analysis software such as TradingView offers powerful charting abilities that allow you to visualize price movements and identify patterns. With its user-friendly interface and extensive features, TradingView is a favorite among traders seeking in-depth analysis. Subscribing to trend analysis reports from reputable market research publications is another valuable resource. These reports provide expert insights into current market conditions, helping you stay informed and make informed decisions. By leveraging these tools and resources, you can increase your ability to identify and capitalize on market trends, positioning yourself for success in the dynamic world of cryptocurrency.

12.3 Timing Your Trades: When to Enter and Exit

Trade timing is crucial in cryptocurrency, where prices fluctuate wildly within minutes. Knowing when to enter or exit a trade can help decipher between a profitable investment and a significant loss. At the base of successful trading lies the concept of optimal entry points. Entering a market at the right time allows you to capitalize on upward price movements, maximizing your potential gains. It's akin to catching a wave at the right moment, riding its momentum to shore. Conversely, strategic exits are equally important. Securing profits or minimizing losses is not just about intuition; it's a calculated decision based on various signals and indicators.

One of the most telling indicators for timing trades is candlestick patterns. These visual representations of price movements over specific time frames provide clues about market sentiment. For instance, a hammer pattern often signals a bullish reversal, suggesting that buyers are gaining control. On the other hand, a shooting star pattern may indicate a bearish reversal, hinting that sellers are taking over. Understanding these patterns can help you anticipate potential market shifts, allowing you to adjust your positions accordingly. Another helpful tool is the Fibonacci retracement levels, which help identify support and resistance. The key Fibonacci ratios can indicate where a price might reverse direction. By understanding these levels, you can set entry and exit points that align with the market's natural ebb and flow.

Various timing techniques can be used in market conditions to optimize trading decisions. Range trading is a technique where traders profit from price oscillations within a defined range. This approach is efficient in stable markets, where prices move predictably between support and resistance levels. Swing trading focuses on capturing gains from short- to medium-term price moves. This strategy requires technical skills to identify potential price swings and the discipline to hold positions until the trend plays out. Breakout and breakdown strategies offer compelling options for those looking to capitalize on decisive market movements. These strategies involve acting on significant price movements and entering trades when prices break through key support or resistance levels. This approach requires swift action and confidence in the market's direction.

To refine your trade timing decisions, leveraging tools that provide real-time insights is invaluable. Automated alerts are a powerful resource, allowing you to set notifications for key price events. These alerts ensure you take advantage of every opportunity, informing you of market shifts even when you're not actively monitoring the charts. Backtesting software offers another layer of analysis. By evaluating the effectiveness of timing strategies against historical data, you can identify what works and what doesn't. This practice lets you fine-tune your approach, ensuring your strategies are grounded in proven methods rather than speculation.

In trading, timing is both an art and a science. Combining technical indicators, strategic techniques, and advanced tools can increase your capability to enter and exit trades at opportune moments. This skill increases your chances of success and builds confidence in your trading decisions, empowering you to navigate the dynamic world of cryptocurrencies with a steady hand. As we conclude this chapter, remember that timing is integral to successful trading. With this knowledge, you are now ready to explore the next chapter, where we will delve into the real-world applications of cryptocurrencies and how they are transforming everyday transactions.

Chapter 13: Interactive Tools and Resources

Imagine stepping into a bustling classroom where the buzz of engagement fills the air and contradicts your typical academic setting. Here, the subject is cryptocurrency, and instead of textbooks, you're armed with interactive tools designed to sharpen your skills and deepen your understanding. In this chapter, you'll find exercises and quizzes that test your knowledge and immerse you in real-world scenarios, transforming abstract concepts into tangible insights.

Exercises and Quizzes: Test Your Crypto-Savvy

To truly grasp the complexities of cryptocurrency, hands-on experience is invaluable. Think of simulated trading exercises as your crypto sandbox. In this space, you can practice trading without the risk of financial loss. Platforms like Binance and eToro offer paper trading accounts where you can experiment with strategies using virtual funds. This approach allows you to understand market dynamics, refine your tactics, and build confidence—

all without staking your actual money. Imagine navigating a market downturn or riding a bullish wave, making decisions that mimic real trading scenarios. Each click and choice becomes a learning moment, preparing you for the real deal.

Beyond trading, portfolio management challenges offer another layer of engagement. Picture yourself as a fund manager tasked with building and managing a hypothetical portfolio. Your goal is to balance risk and reward, considering factors like asset allocation, market conditions, and investment goals. These challenges push you to think strategically, honing skills crucial for effective cryptocurrency management. Each decision that you make mirrors the complexities of managing real investments. Through these exercises, you're not just learning; you're practicing the art of stewardship over digital assets.

Quizzes are a convenient way to assess your understanding of cryptocurrency concepts. Think of these as your personal checkpoints, evaluating your grasp on topics ranging from blockchain fundamentals to the intricacies of tokens. Multiple-choice questions cover essential concepts, ensuring that your foundational knowledge is rock-solid. But the learning continues beyond there. Scenario-based questions present real-world situations, challenging you to apply your knowledge in practical contexts. These scenarios test your problem-solving abilities, asking you to think critically and make proper decisions based on the information. As you successfully navigate these challenges, you'll feel a sense of empowerment and accomplishment from mastering these complex concepts.

Feedback is a crucial component for gaining knowledge. Each quiz provides instant feedback, offering detailed explanations for each answer. Understanding why a particular answer is correct reinforces your expertise and helps solidify your understanding of complex topics. Additionally, standard mistake clarifications address frequent misconceptions, ensuring you memorize facts and truly comprehend the material. This feedback loop is essential for growth, turning each quiz into a learning opportunity that builds upon your knowledge.

As you engage with these interactive elements, progress-tracking features provide a comprehensive view of your development. Score tracking allows you to monitor your performance over time, highlighting areas where you've excelled and those that may need more focus. Skill-level assessments categorize your proficiency into beginner, intermediate, and advanced tiers, offering a clear roadmap for your learning journey. This structured approach ensures that you're always aware of your progress, empowering you to take control of your education and tailor your efforts to your specific needs. You'll feel a sense of direction and control as you navigate your learning journey.

Interactive Element: Crypto Case Study

Consider a case study in which you manage a virtual portfolio during a period of market volatility. In this case study, you'll be presented with a series of market events and given the opportunity to make decisions based on your understanding of cryptocurrency. You'll then be able to analyze how these events impact your decisions and reflect on the outcomes. Use this exercise to identify areas for improvement and strategies that worked well. By doing so, you can enhance your understanding and prepare yourself for navigating real market challenges with confidence and strategy.

Resource Lists: Tools and Platforms for Continued Learning

Navigating the world of cryptocurrency can feel like stepping into a vast library, each book holding secrets to financial empowerment. To help you decode these mysteries, let's start with educational platforms. Websites like Coursera and edX offer structured courses on blockchain technology, providing a solid foundation in the mechanics of digital currencies. These platforms are ideal if you prefer a guided learning experience with a curriculum designed by experts. In addition, YouTube offers a wealth of video tutorials from crypto influencers who share insights and strategies in an engaging, visual format. This medium is perfect for visual learners who want to see concepts in action and hear directly from industry practitioners. Whether listening to a lecture or watching a live trade, these resources bring the crypto world to life, making complex ideas accessible.

For those who enjoy diving into books, several essential readings can deepen your understanding of cryptocurrency. "Mastering Bitcoin" by Andreas M. Antonopoulos is a must-read. This book is a comprehensive guide to Bitcoin, breaking down its technical aspects in an easy-to-understand manner. It's perfect for anyone who wants to grasp the intricacies of how Bitcoin operates. Another insightful read is "The Bitcoin Standard" by Saifedean Ammous. This book offers an economic perspective on Bitcoin, exploring its potential to replace traditional financial systems. Both books provide valuable insights into cryptocurrencies' underlying principles and potential impact, setting a solid foundation for your crypto knowledge.

Effective management and analysis of your crypto investments require the right tools. Portfolio trackers like CoinStats allow you to monitor asset performance across multiple exchanges, giving you a clear overview of your holdings and their current value. This utility is invaluable for making informed decisions about buying, selling, or holding assets. Similarly, platforms like TradingView offer advanced charting tools for those interested in technical analysis to study price movements and trends. These tools provide a wealth of data and indicators to identify potential entry and exit points, enhancing your trading strategy and investment decisions.

Staying abreast of the latest developments in the crypto world is crucial. Reliable news sources like CoinDesk and Cointelegraph provide:

- Up-to-the-minute industry updates.

- Offering insights into market trends.

- Regulatory changes.

- Technological advancements.

These sites are essential for keeping your finger on the pulse of the crypto space, helping you anticipate shifts and make timely decisions. By staying informed about the latest developments, you'll feel a sense of anticipation and preparedness, ready to navigate any market changes. Reliable news sources like CoinDesk and Cointelegraph provide: Up-to-the-minute industry updates. Offering insights into market trends. Regulatory changes. Technological advancements.

Building a Support Network: Community and Forums

Stepping into the cryptocurrency world can be overwhelming, but connecting with others can make it more accessible and enriching. Engaging with online crypto communities is a great way to start. Platforms like Reddit offer a plethora of subreddits dedicated to cryptocurrency discussions. These spaces are bustling with news, debates, and insights shared by people from all walks of life. Whether a beginner or a seasoned trader, these forums allow you to learn, ask questions, and gain different perspectives on the latest trends and developments. Engaging in these discussions can deepen your understanding of complex topics and help you see things from various angles.

Telegram and Discord groups take this engagement to another level by offering real-time chat and collaboration opportunities. These platforms host numerous groups where you can interact directly with other crypto enthusiasts, developers, and even industry insiders. The immediacy of these platforms means you can participate in dynamic discussions, exchange ideas, and get instant feedback. This environment fosters a sense of community to share your experiences and learn from others. It's like having a team of advisors at your fingertips, ready to offer support and guidance whenever needed.

Networking and collaboration are integral components of success in the crypto space. Developing a robust support network can significantly enhance your learning experience. By connecting with others, you open yourself to knowledge exchange, gaining insights from the successes and failures of those around you. These interactions can also lead to collaborative opportunities, where you partner with developers or investors on new projects. Such collaborations can expand your horizons, introduce you to new tools and strategies, and potentially lead to profitable ventures. The relationships you build can provide a safety net of advice and encouragement, helping you navigate the often volatile crypto markets.

Mentorship plays a vital role in this process. Learning from someone more experienced can accelerate your growth and help you avoid common pitfalls. Finding a mentor in the crypto community might seem daunting, but there are several ways to go about it. Look for active individuals in the forums and groups you frequent, consistently offering valuable advice and insights. Reach out to them with respect and genuine interest, expressing your desire to learn and grow. Mentorship platforms were designed to connect mentors and mentees, offering structured programs to foster these relationships. A good mentor can provide personalized guidance, helping you set and achieve your crypto goals.

As you engage with these communities, it's essential to maintain a positive and secure presence. Community etiquette should always be at the forefront of your interactions. Communicate respectfully, offering constructive feedback, and acknowledging different viewpoints. This approach fosters a supportive environment and enhances your reputation within the community. Equally important is safeguarding your privacy. Protect your personal information and digital identity by being cautious about what you share. Use secure communication channels, and be wary of unsolicited requests for information. By following these practices, you can enjoy the benefits of community engagement while keeping your online presence safe and respected.

This chapter explores the immense value of building a support network within the crypto community. Participating in online forums, engaging in real-time discussions, and seeking mentorship can enrich your learning experience and enhance your crypto journey. These connections provide knowledge, support, and opportunities that can significantly impact your success. As we move forward, we'll delve into the practical aspects of integrating cryptocurrencies into your everyday life to help increase your financial portfolio by diversifying and building your digital assets.

Chapter 14: Emphasizing Security and Trust

Imagine walking into a village market where every stallholder knows their neighbor. In this market, trust is the currency that keeps business flowing smoothly. Much like this bustling scene, the cryptocurrency ecosystem thrives on trust. Yet, unlike the physical world, where you can look someone in the eye, digital interactions require new forms of trust. This trust isn't about blind faith in any single entity but rather confidence in the systems and communities that underpin the crypto world, where trust is built through transparency, peer reviews, and the decentralized nature of blockchain technology, which minimizes the need for intermediaries. Understanding the role of trust in cryptocurrency is foundational for anyone looking to engage with digital assets.

Community reliability is the cornerstone of the crypto space. It's the bedrock for trust, creating an environment where information and insights are freely shared. Peer reviews and community endorsements play a pivotal role in this context. These are mechanisms where members of the community evaluate and recommend projects, exchanges, and services based on their experiences and knowledge. They are similar to customer reviews that guide us when making online purchases. Platforms like Reddit and Bitcointalk are invaluable resources for these discussions, offering a space where enthusiasts and experts alike can share experiences and advice. These forums act as a collective knowledge base, allowing you to tap into the crowd's wisdom. Industry conferences such as Consensus and Blockchain Expo provide opportunities to engage directly with thought leaders and innovators, further building your understanding and network.

Blockchain technology introduces the concept of trustless systems, a term that might sound counterintuitive but is revolutionary in its implications. In a traditional financial system, trust is placed in centralized entities like banks or government institutions to manage and secure transactions. In contrast, blockchain decentralizes this trust, distributing it across a network of participants. This means that you don't need to trust any single entity to ensure the security and validity of transactions. Instead, the system itself, through its design and the consensus of its participants, ensures the integrity of transactions. This system reduces the risk of fraud and manipulation, as every transaction is recorded on a public ledger that is immutable and transparent. More importantly, blockchain technology enables transactions without needing a trusted third party, empowering you with control over your financial interactions and facilitating a significant shift from conventional systems, aligning with the crypto ethos of independence and self-reliance.

Finding reputable community platforms is essential for navigating the crypto landscape effectively. With its subreddits like r/CryptoCurrency and r/Bitcoin, Reddit offers a wealth of information and discussion on various topics. These communities are vibrant and dynamic, constantly evolving with the latest trends and insights. Bitcointalk, one of the oldest forums dedicated to cryptocurrency, is another valuable platform where you can engage with seasoned investors and developers. Participating in these forums enhances your knowledge and connects you with a broader network of crypto enthusiasts. Engaging with credible sources helps filter out noise and misinformation, providing a more straightforward path to informed decision-making.

Following influential thought leaders and engaging with them can transform your understanding of the crypto world. Twitter is a powerful tool for this purpose, offering real-time updates from key figures like Andreas M. Antonopoulos, renowned for his Bitcoin and blockchain technology expertise. Podcasts such as "Unchained" by Laura Shin provide in-depth discussions and interviews with industry leaders, offering insights into emerging trends and technologies. These platforms allow you to learn from those who have navigated the complexities of cryptocurrency, providing valuable perspectives that can shape your approach and strategy.

Sustaining a culture of transparency and integrity within the crypto ecosystem is crucial for building trust and ensuring long-term success. As a member of this community, your role is integral. Supporting open-source projects is one way to contribute to this culture. Open-source projects are those that make their source code available for anybody to inspect, modify, and enhance. These projects prioritize transparent development practices and collaborative innovation. Examples of such projects in the crypto space include Bitcoin, Ethereum, and many others. Open-source projects invite scrutiny and improvement from the community, ensuring that the technology evolves with the collective input of its users. Honest discourse is equally essential, encouraging constructive discussions and exchanging ideas. You contribute to a more trustworthy and robust crypto ecosystem by prioritizing transparency and integrity in your interactions.

Interactive Element: Reflection Section

Consider your role in the crypto community. Reflect on how you can contribute to a culture of trust and transparency. List ways to engage with reputable platforms, follow thought leaders and support open-source projects. Consider how these actions can enhance your understanding and involvement in cryptocurrency.

14.2 Advanced Security Measures: Beyond the Basics

When securing your cryptocurrency, there might need to be more than just relying on basic measures. The stakes are high, and the need for robust security protocols is paramount. One advanced method you can employ is using multi-signature wallets, which need more than one signature to authorize a transaction, adding extra layers of security. Imagine a vault that requires multiple keys to open; this is how a multi-signature wallet works. It divides control among trusted parties, meaning that no single individual has the power to transfer funds unilaterally. This setup protects against unauthorized access and ensures that the funds remain safe if one key is compromised, as additional signatures are needed to complete any transaction.

Cold storage options offer another level of security by keeping your digital assets offline. These methods are particularly effective for safeguarding extensive holdings. Air-gapped devices are a popular choice. They are never connected to the internet, making them immune to online hacking attempts. Such devices store your private keys securely, protecting your assets from cyber threats.

On the other hand, paper wallets—physical pieces of paper where your private and public keys are printed—provide a simple yet effective form of cold storage. By generating keys offline, you eliminate the risk of exposure to malware or phishing attacks. However, the physical security of the paper wallet becomes crucial, as losing it means losing access to your funds.

Hardware Security Modules (HSMs) take security further by providing a physical device that protects cryptographic keys. These devices are used to securely store and manage private keys, offering a tamper-proof environment significantly reducing the risk of unauthorized access. HSMs also excel in data encryption, safeguarding sensitive information from potential breaches. With an accumulating sophistication of cyber threats, ensuring that your cryptographic keys are well-protected is non-negotiable. HSMs provide peace of mind by offering a robust key management and data encryption solution, making them indispensable for those serious about security.

Staying informed about emerging security threats is vital in the fast-paced world of cryptocurrency. Social engineering attacks, which prey on human psychology rather than technological vulnerabilities, are rising. These attacks often involve manipulation tactics to trick individuals into revealing sensitive information. Knowing these tactics is crucial for safeguarding your assets. Zero-day vulnerabilities, or security flaws exploited before developers can release a fix, pose another significant threat. Understanding these vulnerabilities and updating your systems with the newest patches is critical to protect against potential exploits. By staying vigilant and informed, you can better anticipate and counteract these evolving threats, ensuring you are always prepared and cautious.

Interactive Element: Security Checklist

Consider implementing a security checklist to protect your digital assets further. Include steps such as enabling multi-signature for transactions, using air-gapped devices for secure storage, and regularly updating your knowledge on emerging threats. Keep this checklist easily accessible and review it frequently to ensure you are following best practices. This proactive approach can fortify your defenses against potential security breaches.

14.3 Trustworthy Sources: Where to Get Reliable Information

Navigating the crypto landscape requires a steady compass, and information is that guiding force in the digital age. However, not all information is created equal. Sorting through the noise to find reliable and accurate news can be challenging. Enter CoinDesk and Cointelegraph. These platforms stand at the forefront of crypto news, offering timely and comprehensive updates and covering everything from market trends to regulatory changes, providing insights that help you make informed decisions. The Block is another essential resource renowned for its in-depth analysis and market insights. Unlike generalized news outlets, these platforms focus exclusively on the crypto and blockchain sectors, ensuring their content is relevant and specialized. By regularly consulting these trusted sources, you can stay on top of the latest developments and maintain a well-rounded view of the ever-evolving market landscape instead of relying on news articles. In crypto, where data drives decisions, blockchain analytics tools are indispensable. Glassnode, for instance, offers market intelligence through on-chain analytics, allowing you to track and verify transaction data precisely. This tool helps you understand network activity, providing a clearer picture of market dynamics. Similarly, Chainalysis is a blockchain data platform that specializes in tracking transactions. It offers insights into the flow of funds across the blockchain, which can be crucial for spotting trends and potential red flags. These analytics tools empower you to verify information independently rather than relying solely on third-party interpretations. By leveraging these resources, you gain a more nuanced understanding of the crypto market, enhancing your ability to act strategically.

Academic research and publications provide another layer of depth to your understanding of blockchain technology. For example, the MIT Digital Currency Initiative conducts cutting-edge research on cryptocurrencies and blockchain. Their work offers a scholarly perspective on the technological and economic implications of digital currencies. Peer-reviewed journals like "Ledger" also publish articles that delve into the complexities of blockchain systems. These academic sources complement your practical knowledge with theoretical insights, helping you appreciate the broader impact of blockchain on society. By engaging with this research, you expand your knowledge and gain a critical lens through which to evaluate new developments and innovations.

In the digital age, information is abundant, but accuracy is key. Verifying information through multiple channels is essential for maintaining a clear and accurate understanding of the crypto space. Fact-checking becomes a crucial practice, where you compare reports from different news outlets to ensure consistency and credibility. This cross-referencing helps you filter out misinformation and biases, allowing you to form a well-informed opinion. Community feedback also plays a significant role in this process. Platforms like Reddit provide a space for discussing and dissecting news, offering diverse perspectives from other crypto enthusiasts and experts. By consulting these communities, you tap into a collective knowledge pool, enriching your understanding and enabling you to make better-informed decisions.

At this point, it's essential to recognize that the crypto world is not static. It is an ever-changing environment where new technologies, regulations, and market dynamics constantly emerge. Staying informed and adaptable becomes crucial as you immerse yourself in this space. The sources and tools mentioned give you the foundation to navigate this complexity with confidence and insight. They equip you with the knowledge needed to engage effectively with digital assets, whether evaluating a new investment, considering a technological innovation, or assessing broader market trends. As you advance in your crypto endeavors, these resources will serve as your trusted allies, leading you through the contests and opportunities that lie ahead. In the next chapter, we will transition from understanding to action, exploring how to build and manage a cryptocurrency portfolio that aligns with your financial goals and risk tolerance.

Chapter 15: Financial Independence Through Crypto

Imagine a world where your financial future isn't tethered to the traditional 9-to-5 grind but is instead fueled by the innovative potential of cryptocurrency. This isn't a distant fantasy; it's a realistic pursuit of financial independence in today's digital age. Cryptocurrencies are redefining how we think about wealth and stability, offering a new path to financial freedom. Unlike conventional investments, digital currencies provide unique opportunities for passive income and wealth preservation, enabling you to create sustainable financial streams with minimal effort. Financial independence in crypto revolves around leveraging these opportunities to achieve autonomy over your financial life.

One of the most compelling aspects of cryptocurrencies is their ability to generate passive income. Participating in activities like staking, yield farming, or lending can earn returns on your holdings without active management. Staking, for instance, allows you to earn rewards by holding specific cryptocurrencies in a wallet, supporting network security and operations in return for periodic payouts. While it requires initial capital, this income stream offers the potential to grow your wealth steadily over time. Meanwhile, the decentralized nature of crypto also makes it a viable hedge against inflation and traditional market fluctuations. As fiat currencies are prone to devaluation over time, diversifying your portfolio with cryptocurrencies can help preserve wealth, protecting your purchasing power in the long run.

A personalized financial independence plan in crypto begins with setting clear, achievable goals. Identify specific financial milestones you wish to reach, such as accumulating a certain amount of savings, acquiring assets, or retiring early. Establish a timeline for each goal, recognizing that cryptocurrencies can offer rapid growth but require patience and strategic planning. Next, assess your resources—both financial and personal. Evaluate the capital you can invest without jeopardizing your financial security, and consider the time and skills you can dedicate to managing your investments. This assessment will guide you in tailoring a plan that aligns with your unique situation, ensuring your financial independence journey is realistic and practical.

Achieving financial independence through crypto demands a significant mindset shift. This involves embracing the inherent risks of crypto investments and cultivating a long-term vision. Unlike traditional markets, cryptocurrencies can be volatile, with prices swinging dramatically. Understanding and accepting this volatility is crucial. Determine your risk tolerance and the level of uncertainty you're comfortable with, and use it to guide your investment choices. It's critical to align your investment choices with your financial goals, focusing on sustained growth rather than quick profits. This mindset, coupled with patience and strategic planning, helps weather market fluctuations and positions you to take advantage of the transformative capacity of digital assets over time.

As you embark on this path, leverage various tools and platforms to streamline your financial planning. Financial planning apps like Mint can help you track spending, set budgets, and monitor progress towards your goals. These tools provide a holistic view of your financial health, allowing for informed decision-making. To manage your crypto portfolio, consider platforms like Delta or Blockfolio. These apps offer real-time tracking of your investments, providing insights into market trends and asset performance. By utilizing these resources, you can maintain an organized approach to your financial independence plan, ensuring that each investment decision aligns with your overarching goals.

Interactive Element: Reflection Section

Take a moment to reflect on your financial aspirations. Jot down your specific goals and timelines, considering your immediate and long-term ambitions. Evaluate your available resources and risk tolerance. How do they shape your approach to investing in cryptocurrencies? This exercise will help you craft a personalized technique that aligns with your unique financial journey.

15.2 Diversifying Income Streams with Crypto

Imagine standing at the epicenter of a bustling digital marketplace where opportunities abound beyond mere trading. Cryptocurrencies offer a vast array of income-generating possibilities, each with its unique advantages and challenges. One such opportunity is yield farming, a concept that might sound complex but is essentially a way to earn interest and additional tokens by providing liquidity to decentralized finance (DeFi) platforms. In simpler terms, it's like depositing money in a digital bank that pays a handsome return for your contribution. Platforms such as Uniswap and Curve have become popular choices for yield farming, allowing users to earn by simply holding their assets within a liquidity pool. This process supports the platform's operations while rewarding participants with a share of the fees and sometimes extra tokens.

Another intriguing opportunity is participating in affiliate programs. Many crypto platforms offer schemes where you can earn commissions by promoting their services. For instance, platforms like Binance and Coinbase have affiliate programs where you can gain a percentage of the trading fees through your referral link sign-ups. This might involve sharing referral links on social media or creating educational content that drives traffic to these platforms. As more people sign up through your links, you earn trading fee percentages or receive bonuses in cryptocurrency. Other platforms like Kraken and Bitfinex also offer similar programs. This approach diversifies your income and leverages your network, turning your influence into tangible financial gains. It's a practical way to combine your passion for crypto with the potential to earn without significant capital investment.

Crypto lending is yet another avenue to explore. You can earn interest over time by lending your digital assets on platforms like Aave or Compound. It's like being a digital bank where you lend your assets and earn interest. This process is akin to traditional banking—except it's decentralized and often yields higher returns. You retain ownership of your assets while they work for you, generating passive income. However, it's essential to understand the risks involved. These include smart contract vulnerabilities, which could lead to loss of funds, and market fluctuations, which could affect your returns or the security of your assets. It's essential to thoroughly research and comprehend these risks before considering this strategy.

Diversifying your income streams with crypto isn't just about maximizing earnings and creating stability and resilience. By depending on multiple sources of income, you reduce the risk of depending on a single investment. This approach spreads your exposure across various opportunities, mitigating potential losses. It also provides a buffer against volatility, ensuring that if one stream underperforms, others can help maintain your overall financial health. The key is to assess each opportunity's risk and return profile, ensuring that your diversification strategy aligns with your financial endeavors and risk tolerance.

For adequate diversification, start by conducting a thorough risk assessment. Evaluate each income stream's potential returns against its associated risks. Consider factors such as market conditions, platform security, and personal expertise. Once you've identified suitable opportunities, implement a rebalancing strategy. Regularly review and adjust your allocation of resources to maintain a balanced portfolio. This ongoing process helps you respond to market changes and optimize your income streams, ensuring they align with your objectives.

Real-world examples highlight the potential of diversified crypto income strategies. Take the case of DeFi enthusiasts who have successfully combined yield farming and staking. By participating in various platforms, they've generated steady returns while contributing to blockchain security. Similarly, crypto influencers have leveraged their expertise to earn through affiliate programs and educational content. They've built a following that generates income and enriches the crypto community by sharing insights and promoting reliable platforms. These stories demonstrate the power of diversification, showcasing how multiple income streams can enhance financial independence in the digital age.

15.3 Aligning Crypto Investments with Your Financial Goals

As you navigate cryptocurrency, aligning your investments with your financial goals becomes a guiding principle. This alignment isn't just about choosing the right coins; it's about ensuring every investment decision serves a greater purpose. You gain clarity and focus by clearly defining what you want to achieve, which is essential in a market known for its volatility. When purpose-driven investments align with long-term objectives, it is easier to stay on course even when the market dips. This strategic approach improves decision-making and helps you avoid impulsive reactions to short-term market changes.

Your financial goals should serve as the foundation for your crypto investment strategy. Start by evaluating your objectives and distinguishing between short-term and long-term objectives. Short-term objectives include saving for a vacation or purchasing new tech, while long-term goals often involve retirement savings or building a substantial portfolio for future generations. Consider your current life stage as well. Are you just starting in your career, or are you nearing retirement? These factors influence your risk tolerance and the investments that make sense. Young adults might be more willing to take risks for higher returns, while those close to retirement may prefer stability and preservation of capital. Adapting your goals based on these circumstances ensures that your investments remain relevant and achievable.

Once you clearly understand your goals, it's time to develop a goal-aligned crypto investment strategy; this begins with asset selection and choosing cryptocurrencies that fit your specific objectives. If you aim for rapid growth, you might focus on emerging altcoins with high potential. Conversely, if stability is your priority, established cryptocurrencies like Bitcoin and Ethereum might be more suitable. Risk management plays a crucial role here. Implement strategies to protect your capital while pursuing your goals. Diversification, stop-loss orders, and regular portfolio reviews are some tools you can use to mitigate risks. You create a resilient investment plan that can withstand market fluctuations by balancing potential rewards with potential hazards.

Monitoring and adjusting your investment plan is a continuous process. Regularly review your portfolio's performance relative to your objectives. Are you on track to meet your long-term and short-term goals? If not, what adjustments are needed? Flexibility is key. Be prepared to adapt your plan as your circumstances or market conditions change; this might involve reallocating resources, re-evaluating risk tolerance, or exploring new investment opportunities. Staying proactive ensures that your investment strategy remains aligned with your evolving goals, maximizing the potential for success.

As we conclude this chapter, remember that aligning your crypto investments with your financial goals is a compelling process that requires both strategic planning and adaptability. The next chapter will explore the broader economic landscape, examining how cryptocurrencies fit into a diversified investment portfolio and contribute to overall financial well-being.

Chapter 16: Bridging the Knowledge Gap

Imagine sitting at the edge of a vast digital frontier, where the world of cryptocurrency unfolds with unparalleled potential. Like any new frontier, it is often misunderstood and surrounded by myths that can cloud judgment and breed skepticism. As you venture into this landscape, separating fact from fiction is crucial. One persistent myth is that cryptocurrency is solely a tool for illegal activities, a narrative that has persisted despite evidence to the contrary. While it's true that some illicit transactions occur, they constitute only a tiny fraction of total crypto activity. A report from Rockwallet highlights that merely 3% of Bitcoin transactions involve:

- Illegal activities.

- Only 3% of Bitcoin transactions are related to illegal activities, so the legitimacy of the remaining 97% is unquestionable. This statistic is a clear testament to the increasing regulation and integration of digital currencies into the worldwide financial system, further diminishing their association with crime.

Another common misconception is that cryptocurrencies need intrinsic value, often compared unfavorably to traditional fiat currencies. Yet, examining the nature of value, we find that most modern currencies, including the U.S. dollar, are not backed by physical assets but by government decree and public trust. Bitcoin, for instance, has built-in scarcity with a capped supply of 21 million coins, offering intrinsic value through its limited availability. This scarcity, akin to precious metals, is one of the reasons investors consider Bitcoin a store of value, similar to gold. As digital assets become more integrated into financial systems worldwide, their perceived value continues to evolve, challenging old notions and inviting new understanding.

Misunderstandings also extend to the technology underpinning cryptocurrencies: blockchain. Many people conflate blockchain with Bitcoin, assuming they are the same. However, while Bitcoin is a cryptocurrency that operates on blockchain technology, blockchain itself is a versatile tool with applications far beyond finance. According to CompTIA, blockchain can support industries such as healthcare, supply chain management, and voting systems. It provides a decentralized, immutable ledger that enhances transparency and security, proving its worth across numerous sectors.

Another misconception about blockchain is its complete anonymity. While public blockchains allow for pseudonymous transactions, they do not entirely obscure identities. Pseudonymous transactions mean that while the parties' identity is not immediately apparent, it can be traced back through the blockchain. In fact, blockchain's transparent nature enables tracking and verifying transactions, striking a balance between privacy and accountability.

Concerns about security and volatility often deter people from engaging with cryptocurrencies; a myth that digital coins can be easily hacked is rooted in misunderstandings of how blockchain technology works. While exchanges and wallets can be vulnerable if not properly secured, the underlying blockchain is inherently robust and secure. Innovations in security, such as multi-signature wallets, hardware security modules, cold storage, and two-factor authentication, offer additional layers of protection, making it increasingly difficult for unauthorized access. Volatility is another hurdle, with many fearing the unpredictable price swings typical of crypto markets. However, volatility also presents opportunities for gains, especially for informed and strategic investors. Understanding market dynamics and leveraging tools like stop-loss orders can help alleviate risks associated with price fluctuations.

To further debunk these myths, consider the growing institutional adoption of cryptocurrencies. Major companies like Tesla and Square have invested in Bitcoin, signaling confidence in its future and legitimizing its role in modern finance. This trend is not isolated. Ethereum and decentralized finance (DeFi) projects have showcased the capacity of blockchain to revolutionize financial services, offering transparent and efficient alternatives to traditional banking. These success narratives highlight the transformative power of digital currencies, reinforcing their credibility and underscoring the importance of informed engagement.

Interactive Element: Myth-Busting Quiz

Challenge your understanding with a short quiz:

1. True or False: Most Bitcoin transactions are related to illegal activities.

2. What provides Bitcoin with intrinsic value?

3. Is blockchain technology limited to financial applications?

4. Can blockchain ensure complete anonymity for users?

5. What are some security measures that protect cryptocurrencies from hacking?

Reflect on these questions and explore how understanding these aspects can enhance your confidence in navigating the crypto landscape.

16.2 Overcoming Skepticism: Building Confidence in Digital Assets

Skepticism towards cryptocurrencies and digital assets often stems from fear of the unknown. Imagine encountering a new technology that promises to upend traditional financial systems but operates on complex and opaque principles. For many, this lack of understanding breeds apprehension. It's easy to shy away from what we don't fully grasp, especially when it involves our hard-earned money. This anxiety is compounded by the negative portrayals in media, where sensationalized stories of scams and volatile price swings dominate headlines. Such narratives paint a picture of a dangerous and unstable market, obscuring the positive developments and innovations beneath the surface.

Despite these hurdles, the crypto space is making significant strides towards building trust and confidence. Regulatory progress is a major factor in this evolution. Around the world, governments and financial institutions are working to establish more explicit legal frameworks for digital currencies. This regulatory clarity protects investors and legitimizes cryptocurrencies as part of the economic system, providing reassurance and security. Technological innovations further bolster this trust. Advances in scalability address early blockchain networks' limitations, making transactions faster and more efficient. Security enhancements, such as improved encryption methods and decentralized finance protocols, are reducing risks and protecting user assets.

Amidst these developments, credible voices in the crypto industry offer balanced perspectives that cut through the noise. Educators and advocates like Andreas M. Antonopoulos have dedicated themselves to demystifying Bitcoin and blockchain technology. Through books, talks, and online platforms, Antonopoulos provides clear explanations that help individuals understand the benefits and potential of these technologies, empowering them with knowledge. Cathie Wood, CEO of ARK Invest, is another influential figure who champions disruptive technologies, including cryptocurrencies. Her firm's strategic investments and commitment to regulatory clarity have contributed to institutional confidence in digital assets. These thought leaders are crucial in bridging the gap between skepticism and informed engagement, offering insights that empower individuals to explore the crypto space confidently.

Engaging directly with the crypto community can help dispel doubts and build confidence. You can connect with others who share your interests and questions by joining online forums and discussions. Reddit and Discord host vibrant communities where users exchange knowledge, experiences, and advice. These spaces allow you to learn from those who have navigated the complexities of digital assets and can offer practical tips and encouragement. Starting with small investments is another effective way to build familiarity and understanding. Allocating a portion of your portfolio to cryptocurrencies gives you hands-on experience without exposing yourself to significant risk. This approach encourages experimentation and learning, helping you build confidence in managing digital assets.

As you explore these avenues, remember that skepticism can be a healthy part of the learning process. It prompts you to ask questions and seek reliable information, ensuring your decisions are well-informed. By understanding the roots of skepticism and embracing the positive developments in crypto, you can transform doubt into confidence and curiosity into knowledge. Doing so opens the door to the opportunities and innovations digital assets offer.

16.3 Continuous Learning: Staying Informed in a Dynamic Market

Consider the world of cryptocurrency as an ever-evolving tapestry, where each thread represents a new development or trend. To navigate this intricate landscape effectively, lifelong learning becomes beneficial and necessary. The crypto market is dynamic, with changes that can happen instantly. Staying informed requires an active effort to understand these shifts and their implications. It means being flexible and ready to adapt your strategies as the market demands. Such adaptability is crucial for seizing opportunities and mitigating risks, ensuring your investments remain sound and informed.

Resources for continued education are plentiful, offering a wealth of knowledge. Online platforms like Coursera and Udemy provide structured courses that delve into blockchain technology, cryptocurrency fundamentals, and more. These courses offer an in-depth encounter into the mechanics of digital assets, providing you with the tools to make informed decisions. Webinars hosted by industry experts also serve as valuable resources, offering insights into current trends and future projections. Podcasts and newsletters are another avenue to consider. They provide timely updates and expert opinions, connecting you to the pulse of the crypto world. Subscribing to a few key sources can ensure you get all the essential development.

Networking and knowledge sharing can significantly enhance your understanding of digital assets. Connecting with others in the crypto community gives you diverse insights and experiences. Consider attending conferences and meetups where industry experts and enthusiasts gather to discuss innovations and challenges. These events offer a platform to engage with leaders and peers, fostering a sense of community and shared learning. Study groups are another excellent way to deepen your understanding. Collaborating with others allows you to tackle complex topics collectively, making the learning process more engaging and effective. The exchange of ideas can often lead to new perspectives and strategies, enriching your crypto experience.

Alongside networking, cultivating a mindset of critical thinking and analysis is invaluable. In an age of information overload, discerning fact from fiction is crucial. Fact-checking becomes necessary, ensuring the information you rely on for investment decisions is accurate and reliable. Evaluating sources for their credibility and reliability should be second nature. Look for evidence-backed claims and reputable authorship when assessing information. Skepticism isn't about doubting everything but rather questioning and verifying before accepting. This analytical approach empowers you to make rightful decisions, safeguarding your investments against misinformation and bias.

As you continue to expand your knowledge and skills, remember that the crypto landscape is vast and varied. Continuous learning isn't a destination but an ongoing process that evolves with the market. You can navigate this exciting domain with confidence and foresight by staying informed and engaged. The next chapter will delve into practical applications of your newfound knowledge, guiding you to implement techniques that coincide with your financial goals and risk tolerance.

Conclusion

As we reach the end of this thrilling journey through the intricate world of cryptocurrency, let's take a moment to reflect on the path we've traveled. From knowing the basics of DeFi to exploring the vibrant ecosystems of altcoins, stablecoins, and NFTs, this book has aimed to demystify the often complex landscape of digital finance. We've navigated through trading strategies tailored to both cautious and daring investors and delved into staking to generate passive income. Along the way, we examined the technological advancements shaping Web3 and the metaverse while discussing the critical importance of security in protecting your digital assets. Each chapter has been crafted to equip you with the knowledge to confidently engage with cryptocurrency and recognize its potential in the modern financial era.

There are many key takeaways from this exploration:

1. The importance of diversification must be balanced. By spreading your investments across various digital assets such as Bitcoin, Ethereum, and other altcoins, you can mitigate risk and increase your potential for returns. Understanding market trends and the

cyclical nature of bull and bear phases can significantly enhance your trading strategy. This awareness, combined with technical analysis, can guide your decisions in flourishing and challenging markets.

The concept of staking, essentially sealing your digital currency to support the operations of a blockchain network, introduces a compelling way to earn rewards while contributing to its security and efficiency. It's an opportunity to let your assets work for you, even as you sleep.

I encourage you to apply what you've learned as you leave these pages. Engage with the crypto community, explore new platforms, and experiment with small investments to gain hands-on experience. Remember, the world of cryptocurrency is dynamic and ever-evolving. Stay informed by following industry news, participating in forums, and continuing your education through courses and resources. Take calculated risks, but ensure they align with your financial goals and risk tolerance. The more you immerse yourself in this space, the more confident you will become in navigating its complexities and opportunities.

Reflecting on my journey, I started trading crypto in May 2021 with a mix of curiosity and caution. The landscape was new and intimidating, yet filled with promise. Over time, I learned the value of patience, the necessity of continuous learning, and the power of community. This book has informed you and inspired you to embark on your own path with a sense of adventure and resilience. The digital future is unfolding rapidly, and by embracing it, you position yourself to thrive in this new era. Remember, the cryptocurrency world is not just about financial gain; it's about being part of a supportive community that shares your curiosity and ambition.

Your journey through cryptocurrency is not just about financial gain; it's about understanding a transformative technology that can reshape our world. Whether you're a young adult just starting or someone nearing retirement looking to diversify, the insights and strategies are tools to help you achieve your financial aspirations. As you integrate these lessons into your life, remember that the journey is as important as the destination. Embrace the challenges, celebrate the victories, and stay curious. The crypto universe is vast and full of potential. It awaits your exploration.

References

- *Decentralized finance: Innovations and challenges*
  https://www.bankofcanada.ca/2023/10/staff-analytical-note-2023-15/

- *10 Popular Altcoins to Watch in 2023*
  https://onetrading.com/blogs/10-popular-altcoins-to-watch-in-2023

- *The regulation of stablecoins in the United States*
  https://www.globallegalinsights.com/practice-areas/blockchain-cryptocurrency-laws-and-regulations/the-regulation-of-stablecoins-in-the-united-states/#:~:text=An%20updated%20version%20of%20the,the%20Senate%20in%20July%202023.text=The%20updated%20bill%20clarified%20that,as%20neither%20commodities%20nor%20securities.

- *Best Crypto Exchanges for Beginners in 2024*
  https://www.bitcoin.com/exchanges/for-beginners/

- *Digital Assets: Cryptocurrencies vs. Crypto Tokens - Gemini*
  https://www.gemini.com/cryptopedia/cryptocurrencies-vs-tokens-difference

- *NFT Use Cases: Beyond Digital Art*
  https://www.morpher.com/blog/nft-use-cases

- *What is Web3 technology (and why is it important)?*
  https://www.mckinsey.com/featured-insights/mckinsey-explainers/what-is-web3

- *Best Crypto Exchanges for Beginners in 2024 - Bitcoin.com*
  https://www.bitcoin.com/exchanges/for-beginners/#:~:text=Look%20for%20platforms%20with%20a,are%20often%20recommended%20for%20beginners.

- *Top Cryptocurrency Exchanges Ranked By Volume*
  https://coinmarketcap.com/rankings/exchanges/

- *Crypto staking: What is it and how much can you earn in …*
  https://www.bankrate.com/investing/crypto-staking/

- *Crypto Wallet Security - A Comprehensive Guide* https://101blockchains.com/crypto-wallet-security/

- *10 Best Technical Analysis Tools for Cryptocurrency* https://stormgain.com/blog/best-technical-analysis-tools-for-cryptocurrency

- *Best Crypto Exchanges & Apps of December 2024* https://www.nerdwallet.com/best/investing/crypto-exchanges-platforms

- *Advanced Techniques to Secure Your Crypto Wallet Safely* https://stellarcyber.ai/beyond-the-basics-advanced-techniques-for-securing-your-crypto-wallet/

- *Kraken vs. Binance: Which Should You Choose? - Investopedia* https://www.investopedia.com/kraken-vs-binance-5189457#:~:text=The%20Binance%20user%20interface%20is,fewer%20options%2C%20such%20as%20Coinbase.

- *What is a phishing attack in crypto, and how to prevent it?* https://cointelegraph.com/learn/articles/wha

t-is-a-phishing-attack-in-crypto-and-how-to-prevent-it

- *Getting started with MetaMask* https://support.metamask.io/getting-started/getting-started-with-metamask/

- *A Complete Overview of Trust Wallet Security* https://trustwallet.com/blog/complete-overview-of-trust-wallet-security#:~:text=State%2Dof%2Dthe%2Dart%20encryption%20%26%20security,-The%20technology%20that&text=Your%20private%20keys%20are%20strongly,a%20tamper%2Dproof%20key%20store.

- *How to Secure Your Crypto Wallet in 2024: 5 Expert Tips* https://www.techopedia.com/how-to-secure-your-crypto-wallet

- *Trust Wallet vs. MetaMask - Cointelegraph* https://cointelegraph.com/learn/articles/trust-wallet-vs-metamask#:~:text=Trust%20Wallet%20has%20a%20more%20straightforward%20user%20interface%20and%20supports,other%20cryptocurrencies%20unsupported%20by%20MetaMask.

- *Proof of Work (PoW) vs. Proof of Stake (PoS)* https://www.coinbase.com/learn/crypto-basics/proof-of-work-pow-vs-proof-of-stake-pos-what-is-the-difference

- *15 Best Crypto Staking Platforms: Top Places to Stake Crypto* https://ninjapromo.io/best-crypto-staking-platforms

- *The Ultimate Guide to How Staking Rewards are ...* https://figment.io/insights/how-are-staking-rewards-calculated/

- *Staking Risks Are Vastly Misunderstood* https://www.nasdaq.com/articles/staking-risks-are-vastly-misunderstood

- *What Are Blockchain Bridges and How Do They Work?* https://www.coindesk.com/learn/what-are-blockchain-bridges-and-how-do-they-work

- *6 best cross-chain bridges in 2023 - TechTarget* https://www.techtarget.com/whatis/feature/The-best-cross-chain-bridges

- *Seven Key Cross-Chain Bridge Vulnerabilities Explained* https://chain.link/education-hub/cross-chain-bridge-vulnerabilities

- *Cross-Chain Interoperability: The Future of Blockchain ...* https://fintechreview.net/cross-chain-interoperability-the-future-of-blockchain-networks/

- *How to Include Crypto in Your Retirement Portfolio* https://money.usnews.com/money/retirement/articles/how-to-include-crypto-in-your-retirement-portfolio

- *6 of the Best Cryptocurrencies to Buy Now* https://money.usnews.com/investing/cryptocurrency/articles/whats-the-best-cryptocurrency-to-buy

- *What Are the Tax Implications of a Bitcoin IRA?* https://koinly.io/blog/bitcoin-ira-tax/

- *Strategies for Building Emotional Resilience in Crypto Investing* https://blog.ueex.com/emotional-resilience-in-crypto-investing/

- *Why is Crypto So Volatile? Understanding Market ...* https://calebandbrown.com/blog/crypto-volatility/

- *FBI Crypto Fraud Report 2023: Crypto Scams Surge 45% ...* https://blog.merklescience.com/general/fbi-crypto-fraud-report-2023-crypto-scams-surge-45-5.6b-lost

- *Securing your wallet - Bitcoin* https://bitcoin.org/en/secure-your-wallet

- *Best Cryptocurrency Exchanges and Platforms for 2024* https://www.bitcoin.com/exchanges/

- *Crypto Trends 2023: Charting the Future of Digital Currency* https://www.linqto.com/blog/crypto-trends/

- *Understanding Web3 And Its Impact On The Internet And Society* https://www.forbes.com/sites/kalinabryant/2024/04/23/understanding-web3-and-its-impact-on-the-internet-and-society/#:~:text=By%20decentralizing%20control%20and%20democratizing,and%20ownership%20in%20digital%20economies.

- *Investing In The Metaverse: A Beginner's Guide* https://www.bankrate.com/investing/how-to-invest-in-metaverse/

- *Role of AI in Crypto Industry - Benefits, Risks and Uses* https://www.tokenmetrics.com/blog/role-of-artificial-intelligence-in-crypto-industry

- *Crypto Technical Analysis: Techniques, Indicators, and ...* https://onetrading.com/blogs/crypto-technical-analysis-techniques-indicators-and-applications

- *76 Stories To Learn About Staking* https://hackernoon.com/76-stories-to-learn-about-staking

- *17 Blockchain Applications and Real-World Use Cases* https://builtin.com/blockchain/blockchain-applications

- *Best Crypto Exchanges & Apps of December 2024* https://www.nerdwallet.com/best/investing/crypto-exchanges-platforms

- *Bull vs Bear Crypto Market: What's the difference and how ...* https://cointelegraph.com/learn/articles/bull-vs-bear-crypto-market-what-is-the-difference-and-how-to-handle-both

- *The Cryptocurrency Market in Transition before and after ...* https://www.mdpi.com/1099-4300/24/9/1317

- *6 Best Crypto Analysis Tools for Investors in 2023* https://www.tokenmetrics.com/blog/crypto-analysis-tools

- *6 Strategies for Timing Your Bitcoin Sale Effectively* https://breetapp.com/blog/6-strategies-for-timing-bitcoin-sales-effectively

- *Best Crypto Paper Trading Apps and How to Practice Trading* https://coingape.com/cryptocurrency-exchanges/best-crypto-paper-trading/

- *The 10 Best Crypto Learn and Earn Platforms in 2024* https://coinledger.io/tools/learn-and-earn-crypto

- *10 Best Crypto Discord Servers & Groups to Join for 2024* https://ninjapromo.io/best-crypto-discord-servers-to-join

- *How to Choose a Crypto Wallet* https://www.bestbuy.com/discover-

learn/how-to-choose-a-crypto-
wallet/pcmcat1639437128824

- *Crypto Security: Best Practices To Protect Digital Assets* https://trakx.io/resources/insights/crypto-security/

- *CoinDesk: Bitcoin, Ethereum, Crypto News and Price Data* https://www.coindesk.com/

- *Top On-Chain Analytics Tools for Informed Crypto Decisions ...* https://coindcx.com/blog/cryptocurrency/top-on-chain-analytics-tools/#:~:text=Some%20of%20the%20most%20popular,cater%20to%20various%20user%20needs.

- *What are the best communities where I can talk with others ...* https://www.quora.com/What-are-the-best-communities-where-I-can-talk-with-others-about-crypto

- *What is Crypto Staking?: Overview, How it Works, & Future* https://www.chainalysis.com/blog/crypto-staking/

- *Best Crypto Exchanges \u0026 Apps of December 2024* https://www.nerdwallet.com/best/investing/crypto-exchanges-platforms

- *How to Connect Trust Wallet to MetaMask?* https://cryptohead.io/how-to-connect-trust-wallet-to-metamask/

- *How to Earn Passive Income Through Crypto* https://www.investopedia.com/passive-income-through-crypto-6386333

- *5 Common Cryptocurrency Myths Busted* https://www.rockwallet.com/blog/5-common-cryptocurrency-myths-busted

- *7 Myths About Blockchain - Busted* https://www.comptia.org/content/infographic/7-myths-about-blockchain-busted

- *Meet the Top Crypto Influencers Shaping the Industry* https://unipayment.io/en/blog/meet-the-top-crypto-influencers-shaping-the-industry/

- *Best Cryptocurrency Courses Online with Certificates [2024]* https://www.coursera.org/courses?query=cryptocurrency

GLOSSARY

A
Address
The Address is a crucial element in cryptocurrency transactions. It's a unique string of characters that functions as a public identifier for receiving cryptocurrency or tokens.
Airdrop
The Airdrop plays a significant role in promoting cryptocurrencies. It involves the distribution of free tokens or cryptocurrency to holders or participants, often as a promotional strategy.
Algorithmic Stablecoin
The Algorithmic Stablecoin is a unique type of stablecoin. Its value is maintained using algorithms and smart contracts rather than traditional reserves.
Altcoin
Any cryptocurrency other than Bitcoin.
AML (Anti-Money Laundering)
Regulations and procedures aimed at preventing the use of cryptocurrency for illicit activities.

B
Block
A unit of data containing a record of transactions, part of a blockchain.
Blockchain
A decentralized digital ledger that records transactions across multiple computers in a secure and tamper-proof.
Burn
The permanent removal of tokens from circulation often reduces supply.

C
Cold Wallet
A cold wallet, a cryptocurrency wallet disassociated from the internet, offers enhanced security, providing you with peace of mind about the safety of your digital assets.
Consensus Mechanism
The method used by blockchain networks to agree on the validity of transactions (e.g., Proof of Work, Proof of Stake).
Cryptography
The practice of secure communication and encryption used in blockchain technology.

D
dApps (Decentralized Applications) Applications that are built on a blockchain, operating without a central authority. These could be anything from games to financial services.
Applications are built on a blockchain, operating without a central authority.
Defi (Decentralized Finance)
Financial systems built on blockchain that operate without intermediaries like banks.
DEX (Decentralized Exchange)
A cryptocurrency exchange that functions without a central authority, allowing peer-to-peer trading.

E
ERC-20
A code for tokens on the Ethereum blockchain, ensuring compatibility across dApps.
Ethereum

A blockchain platform that approves smart contracts and dApps featuring its native currency, Ether (ETH).

EVM (Ethereum Virtual Machine)

The runtime scope for smart contracts on Ethereum.

F

Fiat Currency

Government-issued currency like USD or EUR is not backed by a physical commodity.

Fork

A change or split in a blockchain protocol creates a new version of the blockchain.

G

Gas

A fee is required to execute transactions or smart contracts on a blockchain network, often used in Ethereum.

Genesis Block

The first block in a blockchain.

H

Halving

An event in Bitcoin where mining rewards are reduced by half, typically occurring every four years.

Hash

A unique string of characters representing data is created using a cryptographic algorithm.

I

ICO (Initial Coin Offering)

A fundraising method where new cryptocurrencies or tokens are sold to investors.

Interoperability

The ability of different blockchains or platforms to interact and share data.

L

Ledger

A digital record of transactions forms the basis of a blockchain.

Liquidity Pool

A collection of funds locked in a smart contract to facilitate buying and selling on a decentralized exchange.

M

Metaverse

The metaverse, a virtual, digital world often integrated with blockchain and cryptocurrency, opens up a world of possibilities for ownership and transactions. This potential sparks excitement among enthusiasts, driving innovation and exploration in the field.

Mining

It's a process of validating and adding transactions to a blockchain that is often rewarded with cryptocurrency.

Multi-Signature (Multisig)

A security feature requiring multiple approvals for a transaction.

N

NFT (Non-Fungible Token)

A unique, blockchain-based token representing ownership of a specific digital or physical item.

Node

A computer or device that is part of maintaining a copy of the ledger on the blockchain network

O
Oracle
A service or technology that connects smart contracts to external data sources.
Open Source
Software source code is publicly available and can be altered or shared.

P
Peer-to-Peer (P2P)
A decentralized interaction between users without intermediaries.
Private Key
Your private key, a secure key used to access and manage cryptocurrency funds, is a crucial responsibility that should never be shared. It empowers you and puts you in control of your assets, ensuring their safety and security.
Proof of Stake (PoS)
A consensus mechanism where validators are picked based on the amount of cryptocurrency they hold and stake.
Proof of Work (PoW)
A consensus mechanism requiring miners to solve complex mathematical problems to validate transactions.
S
Satoshi
The smallest unit of Bitcoin is equal to 0.00000001 BTC.
Scalability
The capability of a blockchain to handle increased transaction volume.

Smart Contract
Self-executing code on a blockchain that enforces agreements or conditions.
Stablecoin
A cryptocurrency is designed to maintain a stable value, often pegged to fiat currency or commodities.

T
Token
A digital asset issued on a blockchain represents various utilities, rights, or values.
TPS (Transactions Per Second)
A metric measuring the number of transactions a blockchain can process in one second.

V
Validator
A participant in Proof of Stake systems who validates transactions and aggregates them to the blockchain.
Volatility
The degree of price fluctuation in cryptocurrency markets.

W
Wallet
A tool or software for securely storing, sending, and receiving cryptocurrency.
Web3
The next generation of the internet emphasizes decentralization, blockchain, and user data ownership.
Whitelist

A list of approved participants for an ICO, Airdrop, or other blockchain events. Being on this list makes you part of a community, ensuring you're included in important events and opportunities.

Z

Zero-Knowledge Proof

A cryptographic method where one party proves knowledge of information without revealing the information itself.